This Call We Share

Martha Nelson

BROADMAN PRESS
Nashville, Tennessee

Dewey Decimal Classification: 253.2
Subject heading: MINISTERS' WIVES

Library of Congress Catalog Card Number: 76-29804
Printed in the United States of America

Preface

Here is the book I said I would never write. "We're all so different!" I had exclaimed in resisting the suggestion of a book for wives of men in ministry. I surely was far from being an exemplary pastor's wife.

But then one day, after a year or so of praying for direction as to future writing projects, the idea took root and I felt I could at last treat the subject objectively. Not least among the signposts pointing to my proceeding was the growing concern within our denomination over the pressures experienced by families of men in church-related vocations. Repeatedly I was hearing the observation that the minister's wife is his most important human resource in helping him cope with problems.

Meanwhile, I had not become an "ideal minister's wife," you understand. But I had come to the point where I could live with myself and our congregation without a great deal of insecurity, uncertainty, and self-doubt.

I knew we had suffered enough to be sympathetic, and had enjoyed enough successes to have a sense of satisfaction. I also knew I did not have all the answers. It seems a thousand times I asked the question, "What are the answers?"

My husband Carl has shared so deeply in this work that his name should appear beside mine on the jacket.

We spent many working lunches and countless early morning and late evening hours brainstorming, evaluating, and refining the material included. This man of God who is my husband not only led me to Christ, but he has also taught me most of what I know of our Lord. I am fortunate to have a husband who is sympathetic with my struggles and who continues to help me over the hard places and guide me gently toward maturity.

I am indebted to the public relations personnel at Southwestern, Southern, and New Orleans Baptist seminaries for arranging interviews with faculty members and wives, who were most gracious in fitting me into their busy schedules; to the professional counselors I interviewed, whose insights I value highly; and to the numerous individuals who shared in conversations, letters, and responses to my informal questionnaire. It is impossible to credit all those outstanding communicators within the profession from whom I have picked up ideas and apt phrases that fit my subject so well.

It is my sincere hope that what Carl and I share in these pages will encourage couples in ministry as they seek to develop satisfying and durable relationships, whatever may be involved in the call they share.

MARTHA NELSON

Contents

To
CARL
whose call I share

1

God Called My Husband

"Life is a call to share in the world's making."

"What can we say? How does one sum up, or boil down, the experiences of thirty-one busy years? What shall we share?"

My husband and I were delighted but thoughtful about the invitation from Clarke College.

"Give us something practical," Mrs. Compere urged. "Just talk to us informally. These are students in Dr. Brown's pastoral ministries class and their wives. We want to hear from both of you."

Carl's presentation would come more easily than mine, I thought. I've had my moments of frustration, my uncertainties and anxieties, my tears in the night. Should I share these?

We decided to build our presentation around the theme, "This Call We Share." He spoke first, and unaccustomed as I am to having the last word, I followed.

> His call had come while he was overseas on military duty, a year and a half after our wedding. In fact, he became a Christian while he was in Hawaii. We had been nominal Christians, rather faithful, obedient, and churchgoing—but minus the personal experience of faith in Jesus Christ that makes the big difference.

7

From his first letter describing what had happened to him there in Pearl Harbor, I knew it was no ordinary encounter. As the letters kept coming, I watched his growing fascination with the Word of God. And, while not quite understanding what it was all about, I sensed his great concern for me.

I knew this, though: there was now a different man in my life! Here was a man with a new love and a consuming zeal to know Christ better. And as time went on, I realized that this love was no passing fascination. It was as real as his love for me.

Between the lines of those closely typed, censored V-Mail letters I read another fact: what had happened to him was going to make a big difference in our lives. Without knowing chapter and verse, or even that it was stated in the Bible, I knew deep down that "light hath no fellowship with darkness."

And my heart, breaking already with the wartime separation and heavy with the realization that he might never return to me, was weighted further with the realization that if he did come home, he would not be the same young man I'd embraced those last few moments in that Norfolk, Virginia, rooming house.

Weeks later, after long and careful searching of the Gospels and a great deal of honest doubting, I came to my own personal knowledge of the Savior. Here was the beginning of my preparation for the divine assignment I was to share with my husband.

As weeks stretched into months and over into another year, in that eternity of our separation, he was studying the Word. Before his return home, even before he said it in so many words, I knew. God had called my husband for some special kingdom task.

I was certain when he wrote that he had preached his first sermon aboard ship in Yokohama Bay, his pulpit a stack of packing cases, his congregation the men he'd lived with aboard ship in the Pacific all those months.

That evening, at Clarke College, Carl shared with those young men, also under divine orders, something about his call. The "called" love to talk about it; they company with men like Moses, Isaiah, Moody, Truett, and Graham. There is a certain mystique about the call of God to a man, something beyond the understanding of those who have not had a similar experience. One has spoken of it as that point where "he lost control of the direction of his life and someone else took over." It is a sacred place, a kind of holy of holies in their lives.

"The call of God to each of us is unique. It is very personal," my husband said. "It may come suddenly, like a storm at sea, or it may move in quietly, progressively, like a tide coming in. But sometime, somewhere, somehow, you catch that vision of God; you feel so keenly the human need all about you; God speaks and you answer.

"Initial responses vary: wonder, doubt, uncertainty, sometimes a flat refusal. But then comes surrender and God gets to work readying you for the task he has in mind for you."

Because students often grow weary and at times extremely restless with the slow processes of preparation, Carl emphasized that the call is a call to prepare.

> The first stage of his preparation: those long months aboard ship with time and more time for personal, undirected Bible study. His library, three books I'd sent him: a *Cruden's Concordance*, a *Peloubet's Bible Dictionary*, and a one-volume commentary.
>
> The next two stages, on his return home: college and seminary. The student pastorates which meant doing what he loved best, but also long, hard trips to the country, sleepless Sunday nights on the return (and most often for the children and me, long lonely weekends of waiting).
>
> Preparation meant Greek and Hebrew, research, papers and more papers to write (and for me to type), part-time work to keep bread on the table, long evenings when he studied late, and I fretted alone in our bed.

9

It meant, once when he was very tired, toward the end of those student years, our reversing roles, his assuming more of the parenting, my providing a paycheck.

"It is a call to minister," he pointed out to the students, and he shared the experience that, more than any other, shaped his interpretation of ministry.

On his way to prayer meeting late one afternoon after we moved to Ironton, he stopped by to see Mr. and Mrs. Sutton and their daughter Carrie, all three of them aging and infirm. He had only a few moments, but he made as though he'd settled down for a visit. Then just as he was leaving, Mr. Sutton said, "Pastor, would you help me into the bathroom before you go?"

Feeble as the old man was, he would need help in getting back to bed, so Carl waited and waited, and waited, growing more and more impatient as the seconds ticked away and the minute hand moved over into the prayer meeting time zone.

Then, as he took Mr. Sutton's arm and was leading him back along the hallway, a word from the Lord flashed across his frustration: "Inasmuch as ye have done it to one of the least of these my brethren, ye have done it unto me" (Matt. 25:40). Suddenly he saw the Lord. Carl was ministering to him!

But then, as the students were caught up in the magic of the moment, he matter-of-factly brought them back to another reality of the call.

"It is also a call to administration. The business of equipping the saints demands leadership and direction. With or without the gift of administration, most of God's men today must spend countless hours doing the kind of thing school superintendents and corporation executives do in a day's work. You need to understand this, or you'll be soon disillusioned when you get into the work full-time."

10

There was much more he could have shared, but he concluded by pointing out that he had found his call of God also to be a call to cooperation. Much of his time had been spent in working in close association with other men-in-ministry: men called to careers in church music, youth, education, evangelism, the chaplaincy, and missions. Over the years he had maintained close ties with other ministers and had spent countless hours working with denomination leaders.

"The undeniable successes of our denomination's work affirm the call to cooperate," he said, and then in closing, "The divine call is indispensable to survival. It will keep you secure though the intellectual struggles of your student years. It will see you through the financial struggles, the turmoil of marital and family adjustments. It will steady you when you waver at the inevitable conflicts that occur in our kind of work."

The students, listening intently, bent on catching every crumb of new insight, reminded me of the dead seriousness with which men enter into ministry. They consider it a sacred responsibility.

Fortunately, while God was getting my husband ready for an abrupt change in vocational plans, he was also preparing me. Idealist that I am, the transition was not difficult. The young women of my generation gave little thought to the career choices of our men: we were concerned with getting the awful war behind us and being together, somewhere, anywhere, with them. So, as I waited for his return, I junked my dreams of settling down to a comfortable life close to home folks and the family business and began stashing away as much of our monthly check as possible for the move to student life.

I had no hang-ups about being a pastor's wife, nor on the other hand, had I ever aspired to such a position. My strongest image of a minister's wife was a beautiful, well-groomed woman who wore an eternal smile and a

11

big hat; who gave nice devotionals for young people and then hurried on to her place at the organ. My Latin teacher roomed at the parsonage and once when I went by, I felt a sense of awe as I stepped inside my pastor's home.

Other than that I had few images of women married to pastors. I remember one, sitting alone down front, looking patient and rather tired. Another looking frantic: she had left her children in their beds one evening, only to be followed to church by a little barefooted, pajama-clad figure. And one more, a pleasant woman, not at all fancy, who liked me a lot because I was her son's very favorite "girl" at church.

Most of our Clarke College audience must have had little knowledge of what it is like to be a pastor's wife, for I sensed their eagerness as I rose to speak.

"It's a real challenge for a woman to share with her husband in his calling. *The world waits to see what the two of you will do with it, what it will do to you, and what God will do through you.*"

Does anything special happen to the wife, the sweetheart, the fiancée of the man God calls? I've talked to many, and some say that before they met their husbands they experienced a sense of call to be a pastor's wife. Others felt the call of a church vocation. Still others heard a distinct call to missions. Many of these met their mates on college and seminary campuses.

Some young women, I reminded the singles in the audience, take positive steps to break off their engagements when they learn God has called the man they planned to marry. Others refuse at the outset to get emotionally involved with one of God's called men.

Some wives go along submissively, deferring to their husband's understanding of what God has in mind for the two of them. A few fight it tooth and nail, denying, hanging fiercely to the man they love and the life they've dreamed of, finally coming to a reluctant surrender.

Others wait and wonder how in the world it can possibly work out for them and secretly hope it won't.

The wife of a successful Midwestern pastor confided that she stayed on in postwar France, clinging to her excellent job with the United States consulate, refusing to return to the States with her husband to prepare for the ministry. Three months went by before she surrendered, packed her bags, and followed him. He was waiting with open arms and she says she's never once regretted that giant step of faith.

I talked with a married missionary who declares she never felt a call to missions. But she was married to a man who did, and that meant an emphatic "Me, too!" She was honest, somehow convinced the mission board, and they were appointed. She told me, "I was ready to go with my husband, but I'd have been more than happy to stay in the States had we been turned down because of *him!* But I'd never have forgiven myself if we'd been turned down because of *me!*"

Most foreign missionaries would argue, however: "Well, you may go as a foreign missionary without a sense of personal call but you won't stay without it."

There is no specific word in the Scriptures to guide us in understanding how God deals with the wives of his called-out ones. But whether we are called, prepared, submissive, or stubborn, let's face facts: We do share in this special work of our husbands and it affects us deeply.

Actually, women in all walks of life are deeply affected by their husbands' commitments. What a man does with his life will affect the woman he marries—the way she'll live, where and how, how much money she will have to spend, where their children will grow up, what she'll think about a great deal and what the two will talk about most

13

frequently, whether she'll enjoy or have to endure (in some cases) having kinfolks close by, how she'll be looked upon by the community, and on and on.

We are involved by virtue of marriage. The togetherness of our marital status demands it. And we whose men are in church vocations are affected more than wives of men in most other professions. Church-related work is seldom a job one does neatly during an eight-to-five day, five days a week. It is not the kind of work that can be left in the desk drawer overnight or over a weekend with an answering service and a colleague.

Like other helping professions, the profession of ministry implies that the person is on twenty-four-hour call, available when needed. It is life-encompassing, not only for the called but for his family as well.

The man who accepts a divine assignment like the ministry becomes in a sense a voluntary slave for the Lord. Here, I believe, is the beginning of understanding and adjustment for the wife.

> As a student-wife, I recall experiencing a strange, enveloping feeling one day. Sharing it with my closest friend, I said, "It just came over me the other day that God is going to do something very special with my husband."
>
> I shall never forget her reply. "Of course he is, Martha, God is going to do something special with ALL our husbands."

The man-in-ministry is in no ordinary job. His work is a task to magnify for the simple reason that he is one of God's special servants, given special responsibility for carrying out his purposes here on this earth. All Christians are called, yes, but only a few selected to serve through church-related vocations.

I could have spent my time devotionalizing and would

have enjoyed doing so, as I spoke to the students and their wives. But I was reminded of Mrs. Compere's request: "Give us something practical." So I shared several essentials that I have found the work to demand of the wife.

This divine call the husband experiences is, for the wife, a call to share him. No longer is he his own man. He belongs to another. Life with him is not a two-way relationship. There is an added factor, and one not to be treated casually or with the usual jealousy characteristic of a triangle relationship.

In a very real sense God holds the controlling interest in your lives. From the outset the husband's interpretation of what God has in mind for him will definitely affect all of your life. The husband may even say to you, "*He* is first with me." But amazingly you may find, as I did, that this new love in his life does not lessen but rather increases his love for you.

The move from student life into local church work adds another outer control to a couple's existence. No longer is the man controlled by the demands of the college or seminary; now he becomes responsible to a much more complex institution, the church. God is your supreme point of reference, and now his church becomes a second, and a highly demanding, reference point.

This call of the man-in-ministry is for the wife a call to unique responsibility. Like other wives, we accept the responsibility to love and cherish our husbands, to care for them, to protect them. But the wife of the Christian leader, particularly those in local churches, finds that she assumes additional responsibilities in connection with her husband's work. In many ways the relationship can be likened to that of couples in the thousands of Ma-and-Pa businesses around the world. While we do not hold legal partnership as they do, with our name on the dotted line in a business contract, there's a togetherness required to get the job done. We find ourselves being his receptionist, sounding board, counselor, interpreter, defender, friend—you name it, we've been it! And like any woman working with her husband, we live in close association with the people he serves.

The student-wife soon discovers that the call of a man into ministry is a call to flexibility. One girl in the audience had recently moved from a lovely, all-paid-for home in a city where her husband was well-established in business into a mobile home in a small college town, where they were launching out on a venture of faith.

> I experienced the demand for flexibility as I struggled to adjust to varying cultures as we moved about. Our churches were located in four widely scattered states—one in the open country, one in a county seat town, another in a Midwestern factory town, one in a blue-collar suburb, and yet still another in a fairly affluent suburb, in two of the nation's largest cities, then one in a very small town.

Added to cultural adjustments were those every wife and mother encounters as family life changes from the comparative freedom of childlessness, to the challenges of caring for infants, preschoolers, young children, and teenagers. Then almost without warning, back to the empty nest, and the couple is suddenly alone together once more.

Plus the changes that the years have brought.

Financial requirements and my personal need for activities beyond home and church added another opportunity for flexibility. I went from doing without to making do, to part-time work, then a full-time job, back to homemaking, then to a late-blooming mini-career as a writer, all the while juggling these ventures with my role as wife of a pastor.

The irregular hours of my pastor-husband have been a daily call to flexibility, and the regularly scheduled plus additional meetings related to church life gave rise to continual struggles with both calendar, clock, and kitchen range.

This call we share demands imaginative maneuvering for privacy and family time together. The unscheduled problems of people that inevitably find their way into the pastor's home either by telephone or doorbell bring added need for flexibility. What can you do but drop a long-planned outing when a church member is drawing her last breath? What can you do but forget a quiet evening at home when its tranquillity is broken by the sound of the doorbell and the entrance of a weeping young woman desperate for love and counsel?

Which brings us to another of the demands which the call of a man to minister places upon his wife: the call to certain burden-bearing. It's a rare woman who can withdraw completely from the flow of people-problems and crises that are a normal part of the minister's day.

No less stressful are the burdens of friction and conflict that plague the best of men.

> Some of the conflicts, of course, add humor to an otherwise stressful existence. One woman, for instance, turned on us when our thirteen-year-old daughter decided she was tired of her boyfriend who'd been spending frequent afternoons at our house. This mother was infuriated by her son's rejection. I shall never forget the tirade she launched upon my husband one Monday morning in our living room. Nor the strange crank calls I began receiving daily. To top it all, Carl declared that for months he had to preach with the angry woman making faces at him during every sermon.

The students and their wives roared with laughter as

we related this and other incidents (some just now beginning to acquire a tinge of humor for us).

"To further challenge me," I told our audience, "I have found this call we share to be a call to creativity. I have learned to take what some would call nothing and make something of it. I have learned to juggle the elements of the household furnishings we happen to possess and the houses provided for us and make a home of them."

The relationships which have been mine by virtue of my husband's position have called forth cooperation, understanding, patience, and sometimes long-suffering—qualities which remain submerged in many women for lack of challenge.

Out of them have come creative friendships which have filled my need for companionship in the midst of persons who never dare to be quite themselves around the minister and his wife.

The call has drawn us closer as we have struggled together for creative solutions not only to our personal problems but also the problems of the congregations we have served.

The faces of the young people before us were a study in thoughtfulness as they contemplated the challenges that lay before them. I concluded on a positive note because, like most of us in the work, I would hasten to reassure newcomers to the call that the difficulties are more than offset by the satisfactions that go along with sincerely offered service to God.

"This call we share is a call to joy. I wouldn't swap, if I could, the rich, full life we have known, even with its many unexpected turns, for that of the hometown girl I might have been had God not called my husband. It has been an infinitely interesting, varied, challenging, and rewarding life." And I tried to put into words some of the joys we would never have known but for our answering this call from God.

Our audience stayed late that evening with their questions. Of course we did not have all the answers, but we shared as best we could, hoping to make the way easier for these young couples who will be moving into positions of leadership as we begin to move out.

2

The Changing Scene

> Several years ago our oldest daughter, whose husband is a law enforcement officer, urged me to work with her on a book for police wives, who also live under special stress due to their husbands' work. One of her best friends, the wife of a minister of music, read the manuscript. Her immediate response was, "Why doesn't someone write something for us? No one has ever said anything to us."

Not many years ago, when God called someone, the message was interpreted as a call to preach or be a missionary evangelist. But times have changed, and with the tremendous changes have come challenges for men in ministry to develop and utilize other gifts and skills for meeting human needs. And these men have wives whose lives are also deeply affected by their husbands' career choices.

A listing of alumni activities in a recent seminary bulletin gives a quick picture of all that is going on in the world of ministry today. In addition to the traditional positions of pastor and missionary, some of the graduates since 1960 were working in the following capacities:

Military chaplain . . . counseling psychologist . . . college dean . . . minister of education and administration . . . professor of philosophy . . . associate pastor . . . campus minister . . . seminary public relations director . . . chaplain, juvenile court . . . director of editorial and research services, historical commission . . . minister of music and education . . . writer of Sunday School lesson commentaries . . . minister of education and youth . . . director of association missions . . . professor of religion, state university . . . young adult consultant, denominational level . . . and state secretary of evangelism.

An article in the same bulletin described another ministry now opening up: the ministry to aging persons. Other positions available to seminary graduates at this writing include industrial chaplain, minister of evangelism and outreach, bus director, minister of recreation, business administrator, director of camps and assemblies, kindergarten director, as well as one with the catchall title, "minister of activities." Even now, further needs are beginning to surface which will eventually call for additional specialization.

More and more young people, sensing the hand of God upon their lives, are entering the preparation stage not quite sure what he has in mind for them. Some who have answered the "call to preach" are now on large church staffs, because this was the door that opened upon graduation.

The heaviest demand for additional church staff personnel in our denomination today is for music, youth and religious education specialists in a variety of combinations, with most requests for music-youth directors. One seminary receives calls for four times as many ministers of education as it is presently graduating. The equipping of saints has taken on new importance with fast-changing congregations.

> During my husband's rich and varied ministry, we have observed the changes at close hand. We have seen Sunday change from a quiet day with only an occasional filling station open here-and-there, to a day when even some church members do their weekly grocery shopping. We

have heard the day of rest become noisy as neighbors busily followed their power mowers around the lawns on both sides of the parsonage.

In St. Louis we saw a choir member excuse herself after singing a Sunday morning solo in order to attend a major league game at Busch Stadium. Her husband and children, also church members, were waiting outside with the car's motor running.

In Colorado we watched recreation—skiing in winter and camping the rest of the year—lure lay leaders away from their posts in the Lord's house on Sunday, often without their giving notice.

The turnover in many congregations has created the need for a variety of equippers. Churches with a hundred additions, for instance, have been shocked to find that when the losses by transfer are counted, the congregation has grown by only two! There is a rapid turnover in lay leadership in many churches. In the cities there are a lot more "strangers" in the house of God, persons with no religious background, or with vastly differing doctrines, who require more intensive training for leadership than those who have grown up in a church.

Multitudes of city-dwellers are apathetic toward the church, and churchgoers are often restless. Some are in search of ready-made programs for their youth, but are unwilling to help get them going. Others are out of sorts with life in general, and this affects their church relationships.

We have watched styles change. During the miniskirt era we held our breath as girls in Sunday night choir raised their hemlines 'til they were higher than the choir rail. Then, next thing we knew they were wearing floor-length dresses at A.M. worship. Pantsuits put in their appearance around the church. I knew the times had really changed when our WMU director arrived at a meeting on a bike, in jeans, with a red scarf pulling back her ponytail, and her *Royal Service* in a knapsack on her back.

Not only in the cities, beyond the mainstream of our denominational life, but also back home changes were taking place. Numbers of ministers suffered as they watched their congregations disintegrating beneath their very noses as the racial mix of the community changed or surrounding property went commercial.

Churches were ordaining long-haired deacons. The music took on a strange beat at times. "PTL" was the byword in some groups. Green-covered *Living Bibles* replaced traditional black leather King James Versions.

With family planning, diminishing numbers of pre-schoolers and children were enrolling in Sunday School. More and more senior citizens were showing up at church.

> Returning to the Deep South after twenty-five years, my husband observed that the buckle on the Bible Belt seemed to have slipped a little. In his Sunday morning benediction a pastor interceded for a professional athlete's performance that afternoon. An associational executive committee postponed its regular Sunday afternoon meeting to avoid conflict with the Superbowl game. A city billboard proclaimed a Baptist youth money-making activity, which had across the years been studiously avoided by most Baptist congregations.

Everywhere the day of the "Parson" has passed. ("Parson" is an old French word for "person"—the "Person" of the church.) The man in ministry is no longer the leading citizen of the community (if indeed there is a community). In the past, he may have been the only well-educated man in the congregation; today, even in rural areas, college degrees are common.

He dresses like any businessman. The car he drives may express his personality. It is difficult to pick out his wife from among women in the congregation. His children are as mod as others.

He may as well forget the pedestal on which his counter-parts of the past were placed, for he will meet many who no longer have respect for his position. Yet the very ones who are the least respectful will be first to condemn him if he steps out of line.

> Carl observes that in his early years of ministry men who let slip a bit of profanity in his presence would hasten to apologize. Now, two decades later, they say what they will, without apology, regardless of who is present and how offensive it may be. And he has been shocked repeatedly by the lack of inhibition of some of today's churchgoing women.

As life has speeded up for members of the congregation, the pastor's work has grown more complex. Volunteers have neither time nor training, nor often the commitment to meet needs that are present. Even where volunteers were available, the pastor does not have enough hours in the day to mobilize, train, and direct them in ministry.

> In our move from a small Missouri town to St. Louis, we noticed a drastic increase in the number of persons who called for counseling. A great many were neither members nor immediate prospects for the church, and some, members elsewhere, asked that they be permitted to remain anonymous. Families of our congregation were also expressing needs for help such as we had never before experienced.

Yet, while congregations in metropolitan areas were growing, others located in declining areas were paying huge building debts. Pastors, already too busy and burdened almost to breaking with the problems created by the changing scene, began to search for men who could share with them in providing specialized ministries to a changing congregation and community.

At the same time, in spite of the population move to

24

the cities, our denomination has remained primarily rural. Three out of every four of our churches still have fewer than 300 members. Many of these are hard-pressed to support a pastor adequately. Many have pastors who work at a second job. In Illinois almost half of the Southern Baptist pastors combine pastoring with a secular job. Over half of the pastors in the Fort Worth area, I understand, work to supplement the family income.

Some of us whose husbands have been able to rely totally upon the local church for support may have been guilty of a kind of snobbery about these men who work at another job. Yet many churches would have no pastor otherwise. In a *Baptist Program* article entitled, "Has 'Tent Making' Become a 'No No' for Today's Preachers?" Arthur C. Helton says we should take care before we rate a secularly employed pastor as second-class. He feels seminaries need to be realistic about the fact that numbers of their graduates will be called to churches which pay unrealistic salaries. (One pastor who has tried living at poverty-level says this had worked a tremendous hardship on his wife and four children.) Helton says, "These students need to know the facts, and be prepared with a trade or profession which will enable them to preach the gospel while making a living at something else."

> A friend of ours in Colorado is working hard to bring his ethnic church to self-supporting status. Meanwhile, he has attended a training school of a leading television manufacturer and combines television repair with the ministry, without hampering his work as pastor.

Given the "permission" of his colleagues in ministry, other men called of God might seek out a sideline which would be profitable, yet not so demanding as a full-time secular job working for "the other fellow."

There are some places which will never be reached

without tentmaking preachers, and one wife sets a standard by saying, "It was good enough for Paul, and it's good enough for us."

> During our years in the West we were aware that many families were actually hurting financially as the husband pastored a church which could not pay a living wage. Some went, receiving a salary supplement and trusting the congregation would be able to support a pastor by the time the supplement played out. But many of these churches will likely struggle forever financially. We knew many wives who worked to make it possible for their husbands to give themselves full-time to the ministry. One, a teacher in a small town in Washington, has made it possible for her husband to develop a congregation and provide much of the actual labor in building a place of worship.

All of this has a great deal to do with wives of men in ministry, for his is a call you share very deeply. Your family life-style will be deeply affected by the doors that swing open and shut for your men and by the choices they make as they enter upon a career of ministry.

It is reassuring to hear that many wives are sharing significantly in the decisions of their graduating husbands. No doubt this will be increasingly true as the men come to realize more fully the level at which the wife is called upon to share in the call, and as more and more women preparing for careers make plans to pursue them after marriage.

What has happened in American society has definitely affected the church and its leaders. What is happening to American women is affecting the life-style of Christian leaders, also. The effects of women's liberation has been far-reaching. Inflation has been a determining factor in the move of women, including wives of ministers, into the working world, as has the rising educational level and

26

the career preparation of these women, the smaller family, and the opportunities open to them.

> As I sit here this Monday morning in my office corner of our den, I don't feel guilty because I'm working (and yes, writing is work!). For here in this small Southern town, all the women are busy, many of them with their homes, families, and schools. A number of homemakers attend special interest classes such as floral arranging and cake decorating. Others drive into the nearby city and surrounding towns to their jobs each day, while yet others have small businesses or are employed in one of several local industries. A good many attend one of several colleges within easy driving distance. The wife of our music director drives three-hundred miles weekly to complete degree requirements at a state university. At least three preschool programs in town are kept busy looking after youngsters.
>
> In addition to their primary careers, many of the men maintain farming interests as well. In the summer, when the women are busy freezing vegetables, I am reminded of how hard women have always worked.
>
> This is a busy place to live, and I would be hard-put filling this empty nest chapter of my life without some interest in addition to my church.
>
> It is nine A.M. The chimes from the church ring out. The telephone has settled down, now that people are busy with their daily tasks. My thoughts turn to the homes of other families in ministry.

Wilda Fancher drove her evangelist husband to the airport early Sunday morning. She teaches high school English and journalism and plans to continue teaching until their sons are on their own. She looks forward to the time when she can pursue her writing and other interests and spend more time with her husband.

Kay Harless, a married missionary with a master's degree in rehabilitation nursing, plans her week. With four children ranging in age from two to eleven, she gives priority to keeping their home running smoothly. She helps her husband in his work with youth, a camp program, and the seminary extension program. But she also has her fingers in a few pies of her own. Among her choicest experiences have been the weekly visits she makes with a deeply dedicated Colombian woman with only a second-grade education. "There's no better way to get acquainted with a person than to visit alongside her week after week. Somehow cultural and language barriers come down when two Christian women come together in prayer and service to their Lord."

At one of our seminaries as a graduate student leaves with his briefcase, his wife goes to her part-time job in the business office on campus. She will return home at lunchtime to split the afternoon hours between housekeeping and her studies and then head for her own classes at the university where she is a second-year law student.

Another young seminary wife, after seeing two preteens off to school, walks to the campus cafeteria where she is a food service staff member. On Wednesday she serves one of the city's churches as coordinator of the evening meal. Her husband, in addition to his studies, works as a security guard.

The wife of a minister of youth in one city plans her week not only to include home responsibilities and activities in their large church, but her work as an interior decorator as well. Her husband is one of the first generation of ministers of youth to face the decision about where one goes as he looks back on his prime years in youth work. He plans to resign his position when he is forty and go into real estate. His wife's expertise as a decorator will be an asset in his second career. They plan to continue working with young people, but in a volunteer capacity in another church.

In a spreading suburb not far away the young wife of a pastor spends her morning with their two preschoolers. Her time is well filled with the children, homemaking, and hobbies. She has just returned from a denominational assembly where she received training as a specialist in Children's work. In a few years she may go back to work as an elementary school counselor—that is, if she decides not to spearhead a preschool day-care program in their church.

An open country situation has been the backdrop for Helen Alderman for years. An artist, she would rather be painting than anything. But between opportunities to paint baptistery scenes and other commissioned work, she keeps busy teaching piano, growing flowers and, more recently, teaching art and Bible to high schoolers. Her diversified interests keep her vital and growing.

A big city church has been the rule in the life of Mrs. W. Douglas Hudgins, whose husband served as its pastor and then as state executive secretary. An outstanding Bible teacher, she has also managed to maintain her position as a cellist with the city's symphony orchestra.

Yes, the times are changing. The time was when the minister's wife was so busy with her large family that there was time for little else. In colonial America a few did some teaching; others took in roomers as Abigail Adams did to keep a homeplace together while her husband was away on the nation's business. Such diversity of interests beyond the home, as we find now in the world of women, was unheard of.

The changing life-styles of all Christian women are encouraging signs if you wonder what life will be like when your husband is at last out of school. One thing is for sure, you can forget the pedestal to which wives of ministers have been consigned in the past and focus on all sorts of interesting, fulfilling contributions in the community where you live.

Life-style is a way of telling the world to whom we belong. It's based on values. It's how we dress and how we behave, the kind of ideas and attitudes we have. It is a vehicle through which we express ourselves.

When our hearts are in tune with God, we need not fear the new modes of expression that are opening to us. Mixing and mingling with the rest of the world, we have unparalleled opportunities to express the Christian way.

Maybe this is a part of what our Lord had in mind when he said, "Go ye into all the world."

3

Forget that Pedestal

to be nobody but yourself
in a world which is doing
its best day and night to
make you everybody else
means to fight the hardest
battle which any
human being can
fight and never
stop fighting.

The poet e. e. cummings must have been personally acquainted with his minister's wife!

Being ourselves is not a problem we just *think* we have. If you have been married to a minister for any length of time, very likely a woman has said to you, "I could never be a minister's wife!" You could almost hear her thinking, *You poor thing—condemned forever to being what you're not.*

It is a bad image we have created, I am afraid, and we have got to help stamp it out—this idea that the minister's wife must fit into a certain mold.

We are making progress. Many a wife is going right ahead and being her own person. Congregations are much more accepting of the humanness of their minister and his family these days. In fact, a lot of the pressure some of us feel is more projection than reality. We just *think* it is there.

Mrs. Frank Stagg, a Southern Seminary faculty wife, says to student wives who ask if they can really be themselves: "Of course! God did not call us to be plastic women poured into some preconceived mold. He wants us to be vital, growing persons."

> Too much of my life was spent self-consciously trying to be "the pastor's wife." My sister laughs at a snapshot taken soon after we left seminary. "That's not you, Martha! Look how prim and pious you're trying to look!" It's true, I was trying awfully hard.
>
> There were those who tried to define my role for me. A well-meaning deacon's wife wanted to place me, Barbie doll-fashion, at the side entrance of the church, handshaking a greeting to all who came that way. I was called upon endlessly (or so I interpreted it) to try my hand at this or that at the church.
>
> My husband didn't help matters, either, with his notions about "the pastor's wife." After thirteen years I said to him, "You know, honey, we're both so much happier since we decided to let each other be his and her self."
>
> "Don't give me any credit," he drawled. "I didn't decide. I just gave up on you!"

What a waste for a young woman to spend half a lifetime so uncomfortably!

Being yourself is an individual matter, to be worked on from the inside out. Your background, your husband's ideas and aspirations, and the quality of your marriage relationship will affect how quickly you arrive at that satisfying, gratifying, comfortable condition of being yourself.

Being yourself is a battle but one well worth the effort. For pretending is uncomfortable, and after awhile it becomes painful. It can create resentments. It is nerve-racking. It saps energy and is emotionally depleting. It is wasteful. It can be self-destructive. One woman I talked with declared: "A woman doesn't have a right to fake it. It's not fair to her husband, her children, or the church. It will eventually become a divisive factor. It's better to be honest and say, 'I can't do this, it's tearing me apart. The internal conflicts are killing me.' Hard, yes, but much better than a psychiatric unit in a mental hospital." Thoughtfully, she added, "I've seen too many fall apart."

If you have been around awhile, you have had a few years to try on and take off a number of things in search of yourself. You have learned that some styles of life, like some fashions, are just not "you." You don't feel right in them.

Possibly you are still looking. Like an unhurried shopper in search of exactly the right outfit, you look and look and look (not buying the first thing you try on), and then, suddenly, when you have just about decided you will not find it, there it is! You know it when you see it!

Life is a search for oneself. You find yourself in family and in romantic love, in reading and study and friendships. But what you find before you come to know Jesus are just bits and pieces, all of which begin to fall into place when you meet God in that personal experience of faith. He is the divine centering place around which all that is real within you gathers.

Then you marry a minister—or your husband drops a bomb into your life with the announcement that *God has called*. It's vitally essential that we understand that this is a call to a life of servanthood, not to a pedestal position to which the world looks up in adoration and honor. So, forget that pedestal! The very idea is foreign to the teachings of the Lord.

Granted, we do hold a position, a privileged position in the service of God. We are a long way from being looked upon as just another member of society. But it is a roll-up-the-sleeves-there-is-work-to-be-done position, and it is a wise couple who recognizes this and comes to terms with this actuality. For there is a long row to hoe, and the work is not easy. It is not all lace tablecloths, conventions, and a Sunday-go-to-meeting wardrobe. It is aprons and study and telephone calls and hurry-let's-get-going. It is a call that requires comfortable clothing and walking shoes.

Even though you are on camera when you first arrive at a church, the folks soon get used to you. After a while they just take you for granted, like an old commercial. They are not spending their lives thinking about you!

A missionary Mrs. admitted that on her first furlough she felt very self-conscious. "People made such a to-do over me. They acted like I was something special. It was an uncomfortable feeling. I knew I was not doing anything much different from a pastor's wife here in the States. So I related to people in a kind of uncomfortable way. But this time around I don't feel that way. I've just enjoyed everything and everybody and gone to everything I could—don't want to miss anything! I've just lived it up!"

Surely our God, giver of every good and perfect gift, wants us to know the joy and adventure of it all. But it will never happen unless we forget the pedestal. There is no place for a prima donna in the Lord's church.

When you move to a new place of service, the congregation begins to size you up. But you are so busy sizing up the situation that you do not worry too much about that. What do the employed women do at their jobs? What are the assets of the congregation, the needs, the liabilities? What about the community? What is happening in the world that is affecting these families? Ellen Jones, a faculty wife who works with Southern Seminary wives, emphasizes the importance of community and world awareness.

The wife of a pastor in an open country church pointed out how very important it is to settle into the community, identifying with the people who live there in ways that are natural and comfortable to you.

> When we moved back to Mississippi, my husband looked forward to having a garden. One of the men saw to it that a spot was ready for planting when we arrived that May. We had to hurry to get it started before the heat of summer. Folks, looking on, saw that we loved the land and weren't afraid to get our hands dirty and they decided "we'd do." A pastor friend remarked that Carl's garden was probably the best PR he could have had in our move from city to small town.

A move calls for an inventory. Before the van arrives, there is the mad going through things, deciding what to save and what to discard. When it leaves, there is the studied juggling of possessions, as you try to place them to best advantage in the house you will be calling home. Likewise, you will want to inventory your personal resources. In conference with your husband, you discuss priorities. What have you brought, in terms of know-how, to this situation? How may it best be offered? What needs your primary attention and energy? What about his? How can you help one another in meeting individual and mutual goals?

The view from a minister's home is expansive. The conscientious wife is aware of a great many things that need doing for God. Her conscience is constantly pricked with the appeals her husband and others must necessarily make for helpers with the work of ministry. Being the capable woman that she so often really is, with abilities in organization, supervision, caring, and so on and on,

35

she finds herself responding and responding and responding until suddenly it is all too much for her.

In addition to the obvious work of church, she is often a glorified Girl Friday, handy for helping her husband with whatever needs doing fast. She is his switchboard operator at home, his message center when she is at the church. She is on duty even during social occasions. And when people call and cannot get him, they are likely to say, "Well, you'll do." And unless she is quick on the trigger, she is caught with a monologue that would try the soul of a long-suffering psychiatrist.

Some wives learn only through painful experience that they cannot do everything! Juanita Epperson of Florida said an unhappy woman in their church criticized her for not spending more time visiting the sick and shut-ins.

Juanita did not take the criticism lightly and so for two years she worked at crowding this kind of ministry into an already too-full schedule. She wrote, "I can visit, but I am all-thumbs in a sick room. Mentally and emotionally I was suffering. The conflict was between what I was and what I was trying to be to please a church member."

Then, through new understandings of 1 Corinthians 12 and 1 Peter 4:10-11, she carefully examined her God-given gifts and abilities, making a list of her obvious abilities and those which might be developed. She carefully studied the list to determine if she were using her talents in God's service. Then in a quiet prayer of commitment, she said she simply gave back to God to use as he saw fit the natural and acquired skills which belonged uniquely to her in the strengthening of the church. She acknowledged God's wisdom in gifting. Recognizing that God decides who gets what, she affirmed God's plan that every Christian perform some function as a part of the church.

This was a turning point in Juanita's life as she made

her peace with God about his plan for the people of his church.

Not only must we be realistic about our abilities and our gifts, we have to be realistic about our stamina, our energy, our health, and our nerves! Our sphere of influence is wider than that of the average woman, and this creates extraordinary, unpredictable opportunities and imposes special demands upon our time and energies.

Anita Thorne, a married missionary serving in the Middle East, says she likes to entertain, and it is a good thing, for in that Arab culture you must be prepared at all times for guests. That means a super-clean house, for where she lives the women are so clean, she says, that they pile their furniture in the middle of the floor and scrub with soap, then go over it with water. (Anita told me, "No, I don't do that; being an American woman I know how to deceive the eye.")

Everybody visits and if the missionary goes into a home to invite a family to church, it is expected that in turn the family will return the visit. You never have a guest you do not serve, and usually it is nuts and fruits, cake and coffee.

"We all get tired," Anita admits. "It's a matter of knowing your limitations. If you can work that out, you're OK. But we all overdo before we holler!"

> One of my biggest problems over the years has been in pacing myself. When plans are made, I find they can't always be readjusted. You just go ahead and then you "holler."

Not only do we need to be realistic about our strength, Dr. David Fite of the "For Wives Only" program at Southwestern Seminary believes young wives deserve enough information about the pro's and con's of church-related careers to be realistic in their expectations. Knowing what is par for the course can save at least some of the pain of disappointment.

"You can expect some exciting adventures," he said, "adventures in personal pilgrimage, adventures with people who care, adventures in watching people respond to the gospel, but at the same time it's no perfect world. It's the same world that tried to destroy Jesus when he came. So, on the other hand, you will find some people who will try to disillusion you, people whom you trust who will not trust you back, and some who will betray your trust.

"I wouldn't say it's terrible, it's horrible out there, because it really isn't. It can be highly gratifying, but on the other hand . . . ."

> I have seen both sides. I remember as a student-wife being warned that we would be hurt, but I did not really believe it for many years. When it happened, it nearly broke my heart. It comes very early for some families, though. God must surely give special grace to the young in coping with rejection and even cruelty. Dr. Robert Naylor says God builds special fences around his called-out ones.
>
> But the joys come, too. On my saddest Sunday I answered a ring of our doorbell to find little Mr. Fernandez, the Portuguese baker who belonged to our church, bearing a beautifully decorated birthday cake for me. It had yellow roses on it, I will never forget. Yellow roses still remind me there are no people in the world who are more loved than ministers and their wives.

Being realistic, you will know that in a denomination made up largely of small churches a great many women are going to be wives of ministers in small situations. But small, medium, or large, the opportunities for ministry are there. People's needs are plentiful wherever your husband's call may take you. Being realistic, you can be assured there are drawbacks to every situation. Huge churches, one woman reminded me, are much like big businesses. Little churches are sometimes not businesslike enough. Medium-size churches in some areas suffer turnovers that can be disastrous. A growing church often demands a frantic pace of its staff. Decaying churches can kill a congregation's spirit, and a pastor's. In any church things can be going along great guns, when suddenly, wham!, the devil himself seems to get loose.

We may as well be realistic about the disproportionate income of most men in ministry, compared to others with similar education and professional standing. At a recent pastors' retreat where I led a conference I was surprised at the concern expressed by the men over their financial responsibility. What a major burden this is for the man with a growing family!

> For years we never had any money to spare. Our Christmases were terribly lean. But we were able to maintain a good credit rating.
>
> Only in recent years have I known what it is to walk into a dime store and shop around—you know, for odds and ends that are not on your shopping list. Looking back, I realize we were comparatively hard-pressed much of the time, but nobody told us we were poor. I do not know how we would have managed if the dollar had been as inflated as it is today.

A young wife wrote that their income had affected their relationship with their families. "In terms of new homes, cars, etc., we do not do as well as they, and they feel we are suffering, that we could be doing so much 'better' in another vocation. It is hard to enjoy family get-togethers; they act as though we are different. I feel closer to some of the church members than my own family."

> We, too, have relatives and friends much more affluent than we. But I believe I am being totally honest when I say we would not swap places with them. God blesses his servants with rewards that money cannot buy.

Another fact of life for the minister's family is that we are called to share our lives with so many persons. People can be highly unpredictable.

Those who come on strong at first may be the first to turn on you when things do not go to suit them. In one church a member who had served on the pulpit committee (and spoken glowingly of the marvelous experience he had had in seeking God's man for his church) made a motion not too many months later that the pastor be dismissed and "two young men employed for the same amount of money."

A young insurance salesman who had been a church member long enough to know better remarked that he felt a pastor should be paid like a salesman, on commission—so much for so many souls, I suppose you would say.

A Wyoming wife told me two women of her church visited her one afternoon to inform her that they were praying her husband would be called to some other situation! What an exposé might be written of all the inhumane, underhanded things that go on—in the Lord's church, of all places.

But for every one of these characters who commit such outrages against God's decent and honorable servants there are hundreds who would not harm a flea. Many are apathetic, it is true, but the big majority by far are kind and gentle and good. Sadly, the finest spirited persons in a church may be the least vocal. They cannot always be depended on to stand up and speak out for what they know to be right.

Being realistic, we know we can expect some suffering. Over the centuries God's men and their families have suffered at the hands of evil men (and some of them within the church). But every profession has its hazards, its hurts, its good, and its bad.

> In our study of law enforcement families I was amazed at the similarities of the problems of these families to those in our profession. Wives' lack of personal identity, adverse public opinion, rivalries between colleagues, inequitable compensation, long and uncertain hours, favoritism, stress, etc.

"It's not just professionals in servant roles who have problems," Mynette Drumwright, a Southwestern faculty wife, reminds us. "Women whose husbands are in other lines of work have their problems, too. This is life. So remember, what happens to you in the framework of your church relationships is not something God is doing to his chosen to take the joy out of living. It's just life. That's the way it is. One thing to cope with after another. We in the Lord's work are fortunate, really, because there are some tremendous rewards to offset the hardships."

Dr. Wade Rowatt of Southern Seminary explained, "I think we in church work tend to experience the disillusionments and disappointments more deeply than lay persons. But bitter as it can be, it's not as bad as the business world. I've worked both places, and it's a dog-eat-dog world out there. Conflict is a reality of life! There's not a whole lot of love out in the business world. Not much of a forgiving attitude. The church may have its conflicts, but it is also generous in its love."

So, let's be realistic. Life is a lot easier when we accept the things we cannot change, and there are some things in church-related vocations which, like the poor, will be with us always.

41

Also, we must be responsible. My original plan was to call this chapter, "Be Yourself or Perish." But after a conversation with James Fancher during a revival, I knew that would never do. He had asked a deacon how his church liked their new pastor.

"Well," the deacon confided, "he's awfully young but we think he'll be all right. Some of us were shocked, though, when his wife showed up at our church picnic in hip huggers. We'd never seen a pastor's wife's belly button before!"

Soon after that I read of a pastor's wife who decided she would never let *her* husband's work determine *her* life-style. She boasted she could outswear many who dropped a cussword in her presence. She smoked, liked Scotch on the rocks, and rode a Honda. She was outspoken about people's attitudes ("they don't think our children can possibly be anything but adopted") and believed the best way to change attitudes was simply by being yourself.

Be yourself? I could not recommend it unreservedly. The epitaph might read, "She was herself—and perished. Here lies her husband also."

Christian women have a responsibility to use good taste and to observe the proprieties of our culture. Wives of men in ministry are entrusted with special responsibility to the people of God wherever our husbands serve.

If we are to survive the claims of a demanding world, it is essential that we develop a strong sense of personal responsibility to God, for it is easy to lose one's sense of personal decision-making in all the coming and going of church life. It is a question of motives.

> "I don't know how 'good' I really am," I often said to my husband. At times I pushed myself in giving outward evidence of loyalty to the church for his sake.

> You see, a lot of ministers hate to have to account for the little wife's absence from this meeting or that. One pastor said, "Everyone wants to know, 'Where is your wife? Oh, she isn't feeling well?' and then they keep asking about her the rest of the week, long after her headache has disappeared."
>
> I heard one wife say she never had the feeling of not wanting to go to the church, but at times I have felt like the seven-year-old "PK" who complained, "Chu'ch, chu'ch, chu'ch—that's all we ever do—go to chu'ch."
>
> And like the four-year-old who prayed at the close of a revival meeting, "Dear Lord, we're pooped!"

Dorothy Hughes, whose husband went from a pastorate to area missions work, confirms that many of us may participate more out of a sense of duty than devotion. She called herself "the hovering mother" type in her heyday on Saturdays as she whipped choir, nursery, bulletins, etc., into shape for Sunday. She wrote, "It has been sort of a shock to realize how much of my activity was done only because I thought it was expected of me. I took my small children out many times when they should have been at home and pushed myself into work I did not enjoy. I thought I was helping my husband by being so involved, but I could have been more real help with a quieter home life and a deeper personal walk with the Lord."

The wife of a minister of activities revealed the inner suffering she experienced in battling the matter of personal responsibility. "I felt literally tired from all the things I was doing at church. Then at a retreat, teaching junior high kids how to change a dazed life into a dazzling one, it suddenly dawned on me that I was not in fellowship with God. I was spiritually exhausted. To restore the relationship I had to begin by resigning as many of my responsibilities as possible. I was doing all these good things with no sense of God's leadership; I was performing only out of duty."

Sometimes, as the hymn reminds us, "duty demands it." But too many duty-deeds can crowd out love-deeds, and for that matter just plain loving. Too much duty-boundness can exhaust us and make us bitter and resentful.

I believe the God who tells us to love others as ourselves is saying we have a duty, a responsibility to ourselves also. While it is easier said than done, it is our personal responsibility to discover God's will for us as a ministering Christian. Hopefully, our husbands will move along with us and will help us in understanding God's will for us in the context of our circumstances.

Somewhere between protecting ourselves too carefully and working ourselves into a state of physical exhaustion and spiritual depletion, there is the call to service which comes from our Lord specifically to us.

Stuart Calvert, the wife of an Alabama pastor, has been significantly involved in ministries to delinquent youth for a number of years. In a *Royal Service* article she recounted that one morning the probation officer called to give her the name and address of a teenage girl who needed immediate attention. Stuart made her way down a dirt road to the youth's house. The yard was filled with rusty cans, broken bottles, and soiled rags. The air was thick with the stench of filth. At the edge of the porch she stopped, fists clenched and announced, "No, Lord, I cannot knock on that door. I don't want to know people who live like this!"

She heard the Lord question, "Who are you?"

"I am a Christian homemaker and mother."

"Who are you?"

"I am a busy Baptist."

"Who are you?"

"Lord, when the phone rang, I was reviewing a book for Baptist Women."

"Who are you?"

"Oh, God, I am a sinner saved by grace."

"Yes, and who are you?"

"Lord, I am an empty vessel . . . ."

"I will fill you and use you!"

Stuart says this is just a carbon copy of countless conversations she has had with the Lord about every experience that comes her way, from how she uses her time to the way she handles disappointment.

It is our duty to be responsible women. Surely it is the will of a loving God that we know a sense of satisfaction in our relationships, both with him and the folks who people our lives.

The question of responsibility, for us in particular, revolves largely around involvement: What shall I do? How much? How often?

Prayerful consideration of several questions may help:

● What can I do that will be a part of God's answer to the needs all about me?

● How does this relate to my gifts?

● How will it affect my family and me?

● Is it something where the Father says, "You, there! This is part of the load I want you to carry."

Lord, give me balance.

I need to be real; I'll try to be realistic;
   I know I must be responsible.
Help me always to remember
   that I have the right to be myself
   and the responsibility to be Christian,
   regardless of what anyone may say or think.

4

Focus on Contribution

Last spring in an interview with Nancy Carter of the
Baptist Press I made the remark that ministers' wives
should "forget the pedestal and focus on contribution."
When the statement appeared in print in the state papers,
I took a long hard look at who had spoken. Who was
I to talk about contribution? What did I mean, "focus
on contribution?"

Simply stated, contribution is sharing responsibility with
someone for something. Life, for everyone, is a call to
contribution, a call to share responsibility with others in
the workings of a busy world. Love, it has been said, is
not just two people looking into each other's eyes; it is
two people looking in the same direction; two hearts tug-
ging at the same load.

For many couples in ministry, the tug begins at the
college or seminary level. Now if marriage to any man
is a challenge, marriage to a student is the ultimate test!

My sister-in-law Ann proudly displays the diploma
presented her by the Air War College on the occasion
of her husband's graduation. It reads:
"She has endured the prescribed tortures,
suffered a thousand and one nights in
the presence of genius at work, walked
the last mile of academic agony with her
espoused and has, in general, completed

> the curriculum required for graduation
> with the degree of
> Pushing Hubby Through."
> Her diploma is signed by the commandant.

Three cheers for student-wives! A round of applause for those thousands who have kept bread on the table while hubby kept to his books! A standing ovation for their determination to put him through!

In an article titled, "The Wife: Work, Study and Love," appearing in *The Tie*, these "giants on campus, some only five feet tall," are described with superlatives: "really fantastic secretaries, capability very high, do excellent work, meet our high demands."

The wives work in seminary offices, the library, cafeteria, and book store. The article told of Jennie Boggan, with a master's in history, who combined teaching night classes at the university with a secretarial job at the seminary until she and her husband moved to their church field. She has retained her position as secretary to the director of the physical plant while her husband does graduate work and says, "Working on campus helps me keep up with what's going on. It has helped me share Charlie's education."

Student-wives not only contribute to their husbands' educational goals by working on campus, they make an impact on the community as nurses, teachers, technicians, sales clerks, program designers, social workers, and so on. The director of hospital personnel near a seminary notes what excellent workers student-wives make—"they take their work more seriously than many other employees." A plus for the couple is the reality that involvement beyond the campus adds to the seminary experience.

Being a PHT'ing student-wife is not the easiest, most relaxed way to live and some breathe a huge sigh of relief when that chapter of their lives is closed. On the other hand, it can be hard on the wife when she must resign a job that has become important to her and move to a community where similar opportunities are nonexistent. Many couples, I am told, find they must take a cut in salary with their move from student to professional status. (Don't color all student couples "poor." Some have larger incomes than their professors!)

> When we moved from St. Louis to Denver, I said good-bye to a stimulating position in the public relations office of a national health care association. The church in Colorado "hoped I wouldn't have to work," a suggestion we interpreted to mean I shouldn't go job-hunting. (Later I was told what they really had in mind was to pay my husband adequately so I wouldn't *have* to work.)
>
> I thought I'd go berserk those first few months. Becka, our high school senior, adjusted much better than I!
>
> Looking back, we see the divine plan in my not working, for it pushed me into a search for fulfillment which led to my highly gratifying ministry of writing.

But contribution for student-wives is not limited to employment. Some student couples make a list of their marketable resources and opt for a job for the husband. Some men combine study with both secular work and part-time work on a church staff. A man who is in constant motion may need nothing more desperately than the contribution of a wife who is there when he happens to arrive at home.

Others make long-term investments in the wife's education with an eye to future contribution. This is a wise choice—if it can be managed, faculty members say. They painted a sad picture of highly capable young men who forge ahead in their careers, while the educational gap between husband and wife widens. The gap can be a liability if he is called to a church he can handle, but she cannot. It can be a liability to a marriage, too, for marriage involves compatibility. When there is too great a lag between the intellectual growth of the pair, there is bound to be trouble ahead.

Advantageous as higher education may be, however, it is not the only way.

> While I chalked up a number of college and seminary hours during student days, I passed up altogether too many opportunities for growth: courses I would give anything to have a chance to take today; library resources unmatched in our entire state; programs I would now pay dearly to attend; speakers I would travel far to hear.
>
> But I absorbed a great deal. Seeing what religious education majors were doing, I began my own resource files independently. I read denominational periodicals avidly. And I typed enough papers to have earned a degree by correspondence.

A counselor on one campus said emphatically, "Nothing irritates me more than to have a fellow who's having marital problems suddenly announce, 'Of course, my wife has never been to college. She hasn't got the same educational background that I have.' In all probability the reason she hasn't got it is because she went to work to help put him through.

"I can't stand educational snobbery!" he said, "Why, my wife has never had a formal course in my field of work, but she's as bright as she can be. She's kept up with me, and we're having a great time working together these days.

"So what?" he says to wives without too much formal education. "There are other ways to learn. You don't have to be a holdback."

The eternity of the preparation period is but one short chapter in your life, however. Much as it calls forth from you, it is but the beginning place of a lifetime of sharing. As Dr. Elton Trueblood has said, there are many chapters in life and a woman's life is long enough these days to include a great many things.

> One of the longer chapters of my life is written around our children. For homemaking has been my prime career, mothering its chief emphasis. Most of my life has been spent cooking, keeping house, motivating, training, explaining, and sometimes complaining.
>
> My most meaningful contribution, in fact, may well be realized in the return on that investment of myself in the lives of our children. The three of them, now married, are coping, contributing young women. Only time will tell, and only God may really know, the impact of their lives upon the world.

Still, with the priority most women put on their roles as wives, mothers, and homemakers, and in the midst of an almost hyperactive family life, the wives of most men in ministry have a compulsion to contribute beyond the little world of home. I think it is a valid desire, for God has told us to love others as ourselves—and I see the immediate family as an extension of a woman's self, and "others" as those beyond.

Finding one's outlets for individual contribution beyond the home is a very personal matter. It is sometimes a trial-and-error process. But when you offer yourself in an endeavor that meets another's need as well as your own, you will find a great deal of personal delight and satisfaction in the doing.

> It is difficult for me to understand the young woman who refuses to share in the worklife of her church. To me, this is a part of discipleship. It is something to put the finger on, to point toward, and say to one's personal satisfaction, "Look, here is what I'm doing in the Lord's church right now."
>
> There is a certain security in specializing. For years I have specialized in missions education, first working

with girls, later in the women's organizations. Frankly, I have problems understanding the Baptist woman who is not supportive of Woman's Missionary Union, if not in attendance, at least by her attitude. It has been my primary way of being obedient to the Great Commission. Granted, at times the meetings have been uninspired, but by staying in there and believing in the need for mission effort, I have watched splendid fellowships of interest and concern develop. Out of my participation has come some of my richest experiences in learning, prayer, contribution, and fellowship.

More recently, I have been coordinating an activities ministry for senior citizens. Other wives I know work with music, children, youth, the church library, as church hostess, and in a wide variety of action groups.

There is a satisfaction in throwing your interests and abilities into one primary area. You can study the work, keep up with what is going on, be creative and more effective because you know the work.

A specific involvement gives reason for that "no" you will sooner or later have to say to other things. It helps you be more goal-oriented. It gives you a sense of purpose. It can ease the frustration of being pulled apart by so many things needing to be done, and being able to do none very well. It is easier to control your schedule. It has a stabilizing effect on the family.

But this is not the only way, of course. Your particular personality, gifts, circumstances, and husband may indicate otherwise. Some wives roll up their sleeves and pitch in, doing whatever needs to be done in a spirit of dedication and love that would put others of us to shame.

Mildred Hewlett, a St. Louis pastor's wife, fills a low profile teamworker niche in their church. She wrote me:

"My husband never said to the congregation, 'You called me, not my wife.' He felt his wife should help with the church work. He just said nothing.

"As the children were growing up I worked at keeping our home stable and on schedule, for my husband was always in a hurry. I sort of moved along with our children, working in their age levels. They liked it. This enabled me to serve the Lord, as I wanted to, and keep the children with me, too.

"After they were in college, I just looked around and began to fill in the cracks where I was needed. I'm not seminary trained, I received my education in the school of hard knocks. If I have a gift, it's getting along with people. I thoroughly enjoy coordinating, planning, training, and encouraging. My long suit is enlisting people to work in different areas.

"One day the church gave me the title, 'Program Coordinator.' (No one is jealous of me, for it's an unpaid position, and most people have no idea what I really do.) I have an office at the church which people think is a junkroom—but it really is my workroom. The church provides me with a secretary, who is well-trained enough now that she can take care of routine matters.

"Anything my husband wants done, he tells me and I do it. He really doesn't have any idea of all the oiling of the machinery I do."

What goes on in that church, without a large professional staff, is amazing! The extensive Children's and Youth programs are staffed by volunteers. There is an active group of retirees. Mrs. Hewlett had the joy of instituting a daycare center staffed by paid workers which regularly cares for 100 children.

The Hewletts have a deaf daughter and for twenty-five years the church has worked with the deaf. Mrs. Hewlett says, "Daughter Sally was the prime mover in this, I was just the "propper-upper!"

Last year, when a group of Vietnamese refugees was

brought to the church, she coordinated ministries to meet their needs: English classes, getting them into schools, teaching American ways, and so on. Four had been baptized at the writing of her letter, and day-care for four of the children was provided by the church. "Here again, I am not the leader, just the pusher. The church has elected leaders and English teachers."

How does she do it all? She says, "My husband is my propper-upper. He constantly reminds me not to be in the limelight, just to push, which I do. He is an optimistic type who never says a thing can't be done. That's another reason I keep going.

"It sounds like I run the church. I really don't. I just help keep it running. I have just drifted into this life-style, as you call it. My desire, as we near retirement after thirty-three years in one church, is to leave it so well organized and functioning that it will do much more when we leave.

"If I had any advice to give to the young minister's wife, it would be: Don't dwell on the fact that you are different, or special; just remember you are God's child and should serve him like everyone else." And then she added in closing, "It's sad to think of ministers' wives trained in leadership who do nothing. They must be miserable."

There are thousands of variations in ways wives of men in ministry give needed assistance to their husbands in getting the work of the church accomplished.

I have never served on a church nominating committee but I constantly keep my ear to the ground, picking up signals about the potential for service in persons and putting the right folks in touch with them. It has been rewarding to see what one woman's faith in another, what one expression of encouragement can do, in enabling another to try her wings for the Lord.

> While I had no office at the church, my husband and
> I have spent countless hours brainstorming ways of get-
> ting the job done. He often said, "You're an idea person.
> You'd have made a good educational director." We came
> across a little plaque last summer which he threatened
> to buy for my desk. It read: "Use me in thy work, O
> Lord, especially in an advisory capacity!"

But it is a narrow view of contribution that would limit
its scope to the local church. The church, as Trueblood
reminds us, is not just what goes on in a building on the
corner on Sunday, but what happens when its people get
out into the weekday world.

The increase in numbers of working ministers' wives—
about half in the nation are employed outside the home—is
not so alarming when you consider the fact that wives
of ministers, like other women, have always worked. They
were among the first women schoolteachers in America;
along with other women of the community they cared for
the sick and met the basic human needs for food, clothing,
and shelter. Today many of us go to offices and institutions
to accomplish the complex tasks of caring for people.

Space prevents even the scantiest tribute to the work
done by ministers' wives. It would be a fascinating study
to research and record their contributions in this era of
human history.

Zelma Pattillo, the wife of a Southern Seminary administrator and a professional herself, told me of one who
has very special gifts in working with emotionally handi-
capped children. "It's such a significant ministry and such
fulfilling work to her that I think it would be a shame
for her to have to stay home and take phone calls for
her husband. With her own gifts and abilities she brings
so much healing to the world, and she's so happy in it.
She communicates her commitment about her work to

their congregation."

Take the thousands of these wives out of the schools, offices, and hospitals and there would be a notable loss of Christian influence in the working world. Most working wives would tell you they find more opportunity to minister and practice Christianity out there in the "new community," where so many persons are today, than they ever would have, should they remain at home.

Additionally, they are contributing to their husbands insurance programs because they are being equipped for life in event of his death. As mentioned earlier, some are making it possible for their husbands to further their education, and the salaries of countless wives are keeping their pastor-husbands on duty full time. In many cases, their working is the lesser of what they may view as two evils—extreme financial stress, or the working wife and mother.

But contribution is still more than all this. The contribution of other wives in volunteer capacities beyond the church would make another interesting and extensive study.

Evelyn Stagg spends each Tuesday morning recording college textbooks for the blind. Theology, she reminded me, has its own specialized vocabulary, phrasing and interpretation, and her background equips her uniquely for this type of reading. The day I talked with her she had started a new book, a study of Paul and his theology, which was to go to a man in New York. "This is something I can do, and I feel it means more to the kingdom of God than my attending a meeting at church on this particular morning."

Mrs. Polly Dillard, wife of another Southern Seminary administrator, worked in a church-related vocation for twenty years, heading work for preschoolers at denomination level; then as director of Children's work and kindergarten in a local church; later teaching in the seminary's school of religious education. Today her contribution beyond her home is primarily through her volunteer service as president of the 1000 member Kentucky Association for Children Under Six, her memberships on a community coordinating childcare board and a state task force working in the interest of young children. She continues to maintain her ties with the local church, serving mostly in planning and consultation, on short-term assignment, and as a substitute. "I feel like I'm ministering through my work with the agencies," she said.

Contribution is not always a studied, structured act— planned and prepared and executed according to directions. Like the good Samaritan you come upon a need and you do something to meet it. You don't meditate, size up your resources, take a hard look at your gifts, or even talk it over with your husband. Sometimes you may not even have to talk it over with the Lord, for you already know what he wants you to do.

Louvenia Edge, wife of Southern Seminary's Dr. Findley Edge, is a people-oriented individual who doesn't require the structure of an organization to minister. "Everything finds me," she says. "Oh, for twenty-seven years I worked in Sunday School, and I've done the whole bit. But lately—well, for instance, not long ago I discovered a couple who needed furniture, and for the past couple of months we've been furnishing an apartment from nothing. We've had such fun. That's the way I seem to operate."

Unusual opportunities for ministry often present themselves to wives of pastors.

> On a cold, rainy November Sunday, Carl and I had settled in for a quiet afternoon when the doorbell rang. There stood a kid literally shivering in his boots, his Honda parked in the driveway. He was on his way from

Virginia to Texas, did not need food nor money, just a place to warm up and dry out.

Now we do not make a practice of taking transients into our home—you know how dangerous that can be these days—but sometimes rules are for breaking.

Carl found the boy a jump suit, and I threw his soggy clothing into the dryer and made coffee. Meanwhile the rain had turned to sleet, so Eddie went to church with us that evening. Afterwards, over hot chcolate and crackers, we talked about religion and life, then put him up finest style in our guest room. Next morning we sent him on his way with a good breakfast, some snacks, an extra "five," and a prayer for his safety and his future. We felt like we were saying good-bye to a son, and there was a hint of tears in his farewell.

But then, contribution is not always *doing something;* more often it's *being.* When I decided to approach a publisher about this book, I put in a call one Monday morning to James Clark, then the director at Broadman.

"Yes, I'd encourage you to go ahead," he told me. "In fact, I've been doing a lot of thinking lately about the contribution of wives to their husbands' lives. I could write a book myself about the ways in which Jennie sharpened and enhanced my ministry and how she worked with me in our ministry."

I was deeply moved as he explained that only the week before his wife Jennie had died. He had asked Dr. Grady Cothen, president of the Sunday School Board, to speak at the memorial service, and I wrote Dr. Cothen asking if he would share his remarks with us. He replied:

"They were the response of my heart to the need of a friend. Insofar as I know they were not recorded . . . I tried to make the point that Mrs. Clark was a very large factor in making possible the ministry of Jim. It is not possible for a man who labors for the church or the denomination to carry on his work effectively without the cooperation of his wife.

"She also ministers in a real and effective way who makes possible the ministry of another. Sympathetic understanding, intelligent cooperation, the bearing of personal burdens, the care of the family, interest in the work, and the sharing of him in person, in time and energy, and enthusiasm are all things which the faithful Christian wife of an effective servant of Christ does."

Dr. Cothen went on in his letter to pay tribute to his own wife: "In my own life it would simply not be possible for me to carry the burdens which I have, to do the very extensive traveling which is essential to the job, and to give myself completely to it if it were not for the cooperation and encouragement of my wife. She understands many of the difficulties which I face. She ministers to me by discussing my needs and problems, by praying for me, and by sharing with me in many ways the ministry which I try to carry out."

Anne Davis, assistant professor of social work education at Southern Seminary, added yet another dimension to my concept of contribution: "We have tended as women to be doers and not thinkers. We have gotten so involved in activities that we don't have time to think and be creative and make a woman's contribution to theology. Some parts of the Scripture so lend themselves to a rich interpretation based on a feminine perspective. There are nuances and subtleties in the lives of Mary and Martha a man would never think of, if he lived to be 2,000!

"I believe the minister's wife needs to keep a strong balance between thinking and doing. I would like to see her more as a theological role model for the women in the church than a social role model.

"I think she has carried the 'southern belle' graciousness,

used the right fork, dressed well, handled herself with grace and dignity, but what the church needs now from women is not a finishing school model.

"We need strong, wholesome, healthy, theologically sound women role models. Real people."

"Can she be both?" I asked.

"If she keeps things in perspective . . . ." Miss Davis replied. And then thoughtfully she said, "If I had to pick out three women who really gave me hope as a woman that I had a role in ministry and that in the Kingdom I could be somebody, one would be my mother, scrubbing the church floor, cleaning the church once a month. Another, a woman who came later in my religious experience, was the kind of person who rolled up her sleeves, also. You could tell her values were in the right place. Even though she was rich, you just knew she didn't waste time projecting the gracious Southern lady image. The third was a woman at the seminary—charming, neat, gracious. You could tell that when she got up in the morning her first thought was not 'How am I going to look, how am I going to act? What kind of image am I going to project socially today?' but 'How am I going to make the New Testament alive in my world?' "

Miss Davis went on, "I'm not saying you have to be a hag, but I am saying the women of the church need most of all a woman who can take the gospel of Jesus Christ and interpret it in a woman's thought patterns, giving them a view of the practical applications of biblical truth for a woman's way of life . . . ."

And so I asked myself, What is contribution? Is it picking butter beans and freezing corn? Is it attending a wedding to show regard for a husband's colleague? Stopping to chat with a new grandmother about her precious treasure? Lingering after prayer meeting to reassure a young woman who feels she can never pick up the pieces of her life for God to put back together again?

Is it running down some information for an enthusiastic WMU director? Visiting some newlywed newcomers to our town? Writing a book to encourage other Christian women? Is it taking time to talk a little longer with a recently bereaved neighbor? Or going with a group of senior citizens to an old-time camp meeting? Is it being a sounding board for my husband's upcoming sermon?

If it is, then I have contributed this week to Kingdom causes. Nothing really spectacular, but then, after all, "God is accustomed to working through the partial, little accomplishments of fallible men and women."

5

Stress and the God-called Man

Several years ago when our church was promoting the "Understanding" series of age-level studies, sign-up sheets were posted on a bulletin board. Some prankster added another title, "Understanding Pastors"—and four people signed up before the secretary retrieved it.

If, as surveys indicate, the minister's wife is his most important human resource in helping him cope, she too needs an "understanding" course. Knowing what to wear is good—and how to decorate a home and entertain and give nice devotionals—but understanding the stresses common to the church-related vocational worker is probably much more vital.

As a young wife I had not the slightest notion how a man's work could affect his entire being, no inkling as to how deeply it can affect his family. No one took me behind the scenes in the life of a minister. No one explained the stresses unique to the work. No one helped me label the types of problems we might anticipate.

Not until I worked for a while in the St. Louis-based health care association did I really begin to understand something of what is involved when a group of professional, clerical, production and custodial workers combine with voluntary members to keep an institution running smoothly, progressing toward its avowed goals.

There I saw the rivalries that can develop between colleagues; the lack of consideration sometimes exhibited; the tensions which surface when a piece of work is being evaluated; the uneasiness when efficiency and salaries are reviewed.

There I watched the burden of decision-making taking its toll on high-level executives. I saw men and women trying in vain to produce creative plans and materials in the midst of the mundane movements of an office and thrusting their work into briefcases for after-hours study at home. I observed the frustration of visions dimmed by budgetary and personnel limitations and board members who just did not see it "that way."

And I went home, realizing that I had been so close to, yet so far removed from, my husband's work that I had not really understood him: the reason for the long hours he kept day by day; why he was unusually quiet some days, and irritable others; why at times I could scarcely get his attention even when he was right by my side.

Stress is a fact of life and ministers are not immune. While it can be beneficial, it can also be dangerous. And while we do not want to be overly preoccupied with the problem side of life, I believe it is better to go prepared.

Men in ministry wear at least half a dozen hats. A quick look at the tangle of stresses they can create gives sufficient cause for the wife to be concerned.

But let us look first at the man you know best, the man without his hats. It is remarkable the variety of men God calls. Men whose middle name is "Go." Some who are studious and quiet. Cautious conservative men. Men with wild ideas. Men who are openly emotional. Stolid men. Men with drive, and some who cannot seem to get going. Detail men, and those who cannot be bothered. Sensitive men, tough men. Organization men and some who never get organized in a lifetime. God apparently sees possibilities in them all.

Like you, this man you have married is unique. A conglomerate of assets and liabilities, he has his particular mix of aptitudes, interests, and skills. A dozen other factors combine to make him what he is at any particular point in time.

He is a man with rights—to pursue his devotion to God as he sees the light; to be himself; to live both freely and responsibly among his fellowmen.

He experiences the normal frustrations of life. He feels anger, grief, depression, guilt. He, too, battles sin; pride; lust; self-centeredness; envy.

Like any other person, he wants to be loved and accepted.

He is an incurable idealist. He would like to save the world for his Lord. He hates the sin he sees.

Donning his "parson" hat, man the minister faces a whole congregation of expectations. Still battling the normal insecurities of youth, trying to be man of the house at home, he moves into one of the most exacting and stressful vocations in all the world.

Some folks think it takes a combination of God and Clark Gable to make a perfect preacher. Everybody knows exactly what it takes:

> He preaches exactly twenty minutes, then he sits down. He condemns sin, but never hurts anyone's feelings.
>
> He works from 8 A.M. to 10 P.M. in every type of job, from preaching to custodial service. He makes $60 a week, wears good clothes, buys good books regularly, has a nice family, drives a good car, and gives $30 a week to the church. He also stands ready to contribute to every good work that comes along.
>
> He is twenty-six years old and has been preaching for

thirty years. He is tall and short; thin and heavyset; handsome. He has one brown eye and one blue; hair parted in the middle, left side dark and straight, the right brown and wavy.

He has a burning desire to work with teenagers and spends all of his time with a straight face because he has a sense of humor that keeps him dedicated to his work.

He makes fifteen calls a day on church members, but is never out of the office.[1]

Scarcely is the last "Amen" of the Sunday service breathed when the pastor must begin to think about the next message. Relentlessly, year in and year out, these deadlines come. Yes, he would rather be preaching than anything else in the whole world. But on exactly what and just how? It is risky, laying yourself open to public evaluation; there is risk in telling it like it is; risk in biting (so to speak) the hand that feeds you.

Does he have the raw material required, the stuff sermons are made of? *I've got to keep studying, I can't let up.*

Will inspiration come? *Yes, Lord, that's what I'll preach come Sunday.*

Will there be time for incubation? *Sunday comes so quickly some weeks.*

When will he organize? *It'll preach, man, but I've gotta get it all together.*

He must deliver. *No matter how I feel, how little sleep I got, how cross my wife is. There they sit; people in the pews, faces forward, eyes front, many of them lazy, nonchalant, sleepy people, now giving their nod to God. Courting couples, runabout youngsters accustomed to frequent commercials, foot shufflers, paper shredders, time keepers . . . only a few minutes 'til noon.*

Reality shocks the young minister. *The world is not won in a Sunday. Some folks don't care for my kind of preaching. Some folks just don't care. . . .*

Beneath the tip of the ministerial iceberg, the services of the week, lie people to visit and folks needing help. Their name is legion: the lost, the sick, the sad. Confused, hurting people, families who need a private pastor, men going bankrupt, persons with bizarre sexual problems, neurotics, divorcees, transients, delinquents.

Add to this the ceremonies of life in which he is involved: funerals, weddings, luncheons, graduations. Mix with a crop of new babies, a few battered children, a case of incest, and now and then a suicide. *And hurry now, my family's waiting.* Man the minister leads an emotionally exhausting yo-yo existence.

The call to administration adds its own strain of stresses particularly to the man ill-suited to an executive role. *Mail to go through. Promotion to prepare. That air conditioner. Budget short, must talk to treasurer. Oil the organization, here, there, once more now. Remind the custodian. Talk to staff. My professors didn't tell me about all this.*

Equipping the saints is no snap, either. *Meet. Teach. Meet. Appoint. Meet. Call. Meet. I'm not supposed to do it all myself . . . I'm not supposed to do it all . . . I'm not supposed to . . . I'm not . . . I'm . . . .*

And who adjusts the thermostat?

The minister's wife soon becomes aware of yet other stresses. There's the inevitable power struggle. *The deacons let me know in no uncertain terms . . . .*

And the personality conflict. *He bugs me!*

Telephone tension is a way of life. *People out there night and day and I'm so weary it's hard to care.*

The minister is a crusader. *They told me to be on the cutting edge and look who got cut!*

Like other men he is the family's primary breadwinner. *I love my work but this salary—it's embarrassing. Gas gone up again, car insurance. It isn't fair. My education. It really isn't fair. I'm not in it for the money, God knows . . . but let's be practical. Dare I say it, think it, feel it? The glare is getting to me, can they see the strain?*

You suspect he gets only shallow support from fellowmen in ministry. *Take those Monday morning conferences, with their glowing reports—and silences. My brothers in the Lord. Theological labeling, gossip, envy. God's men on Monday. Bear ye one another's burdens. I'm hurting but do I dare share? The record speaks. But there's no place to put what's happening among my people.*

He's only human, bless him. *I want to run. Why do I have to be responsible, God, for a group of your people? These people don't care. Why shouldn't I get away from it? God, there's nobody left but me—dear God, in my heart I want to be faithful but how I sometimes yearn to get out from under all this. If I moved six inches every time I'd like to resign I'd soon be in the middle of the Pacific! I need to get away—from these people, from me . . . LOOK MAN REMEMBER JEREMIAH!*

If what the men themselves are saying, in interviews, letters to editors, articles, and books is typical, this is but a sampling of the maverick feelings which skitter across the consciousness of many a good minister.

Still, Dr. Albert McClellan, editor of *The Baptist Program*, notes that while the pastorate is a hard job and, according to many, getting harder, there are some men who seem to escape much of the trouble. "They go to the end triumphant, full of good works, and in full favor with the brothers and sisters and even with the young people. They persevere and retire in peace—no regrets, no disappointments, no recrimination, even if they have no money. Their ministry was worth the doing of it."

He notes that these men seem to hold certain things in common: they have an indelible sense of call; they keep growing; they are themselves; they are professionally com-

66

petent; they have happy family situations; and they belong to their fellow ministers.

Not that they have not experienced stress; they have somehow been able to handle it.

It is encouraging to note from an interdenominational survey of some 8,000 ministers that in spite of the frustrations, ninety-three percent agreed with the statement, "Overall, I am very satisfied with being in the ministry."

But it's a well-known fact that a good many pastors are perishing in the parish. Bob Dale, pastoral ministries consultant with the Sunday School Board, notes pastoral dropouts tend to leave the ministry during three predictable crises in their lives. These crises surface when the minister is three to five years out of seminary . . . at around age forty . . . and near the age of sixty. "The first crisis," he notes, "involves his idealism, the second his need to meet increasing family obligations, and the third or preretirement crisis, his lower energy, high experience, and an eagerness to serve when opportunities lag."

Only a cold and uncaring woman could ignore the tensions she sees when God's man, her husband, is caught up in the battles between a dedicated servant of God and the flesh, both his and his fellowman's. "God help this man, your minister," she prays. "Calm, encourage, inspire, motivate, invigorate, renew, reassure, cheer, direct, undergird, fill with your Spirit, envelop my husband with your great love. And Lord, isn't there *something* I can do to help?"

My husband and I are well-acquainted with the stresses common to the work. Together we have walked the valleys of discouragement and uncertainty. We have seen battles lost, but as he reminds me, "A general can lose some battles but still win the war!"

We have shared so deeply and intimately in the work

67

to which he was called that I find it difficult to determine where *his* stresses leave off and *mine* begin.

When the strain was most intense, we have comforted one another, we have given more of ourselves to each other. At times I have been the one who needed the most help in coping, at other times it was he.

In those blinding moments when I was weakest, my husband's calm understanding of my need for expressing hostility and hurt and his quiet mentions of the glories of serving God have seen me through to brighter days.

Once my heart stopped when I heard him say, "I don't know if I can snap back" (one tends to get less resilient with the years). But he did and I thank God.

There were times when, not knowing how else to pray, I prayed, "God, give him one small victory today," and we gloried in the answers.

He says my trust in him, my perspective, and during difficult times, my reassurance that "We're in this thing together," has helped him most of all.

Love is two people walking a path together and comparing notes on what they see. In work as deeply shared as ours, two viewpoints are invaluable.

What he may see as a mountain, you may recognize as nothing more than a molehill. "A hundred years from now, what difference will it make?"

When the little foxes are nibbling away at the fellowship, all he may be able to see for a moment are the holes in the fences. From your perspective you may be able to remind him of the strengths of the congregation. "From the time you are born 'til you ride in a hearse, things are never so bad they couldn't be worse."

When all he can see are the weaknesses of the leadership, you may be the one to remember that the Lord, the very embodiment of a minister's ideals, was most patient, taking individuals at face value, and trying to move them from where they were to where he knew they should be.

"After all, if everyone were perfect, we'd be out of a job!"

When the "this church" and "this people" syndrome strikes, you may be the one who will be reminded that good families have their problems, too. An evangelist, the son of a pastor, said, "The problems are pretty much the same wherever you go, the faces are just different."

When the ego is hurt (and nothing hurts any worse), it is just evidence of the fact that ministers, like their wives, are only human. One young Methodist minister, reassigned to the same charge several times cried out to an elderly steward, "They're crucifying me! They're crucifying me!" The old man's wise reply was, "Yes, Pastor, but you haven't died yet." One counselor says some ministers seem to be going around with hammer and nails just waiting to be crucified.

The Bible does not teach us to invite suffering. It will come uninvited as we go about the business of living. You may have observed that people seem to react adversely to martyr types. They dislike hearing ministers and their wives poor-mouthing about their lack of time, money, cooperation, support, and so on.

Of course, it is largely up to the minister himself to handle, with God's help, the tensions and stresses that beset him. Nor can we expect him to handle ours, as much as we would like to hand them over sometimes. Both of us are responsible for our attitudes. But, recognizing the strong conflict he experiences between good and evil, the wife can have a stabilizing influence. By just being there when she is needed, reflecting upon the cause to which they are committed, and seeing God's hand at work all around, she may help him return to the vision which moved him out beyond himself in the first place. The remembrance of past victories can refresh and renew. The recall of those who have gone before us to make the way better calls us to visions of the future.

> Little visions can sometimes keep us going. One of my favorites has been in seeing tomorrow in the lives of the little girls accepting Christ and becoming involved in the life of the church.
>
> I see them growing up with knowledge of the Lord, maturing, and establishing homes and making them Christian. Because I have seen a thousand sad pictures of homes without the Savior, these little girls give me hope for tomorrow and assurance of the validity of our place in God's plan.

In-church fighting probably causes the most severe tension for couples in church-related work. It is encouraging to know that seminaries are providing studies in conflict within the Christian community and the denomination is offering practical help along this line. Wives could benefit tremendously from such studies too; the worst thing we can do is to push the panic button when conflict rears its ugly head. The minister is having enough professional problems without having to deal with a panicky wife at home.

For instance, it is helpful to realize that some conflicts the minister experiences are not of his making. He has inherited them.

Also, it is helpful to know that, as Dr. Karl Menninger notes, "The clergyman will be both adored and detested *irrationally by some people for reasons not know to him or to them*." He points out that some of the flattery a minister may receive is as completely undeserved and unintentional as the negative reactions are. "The clergyman needs to be warned neither to take it at face value nor to ignore it," he says. "Such misidentifications with other persons are occurring by and to all of us constantly. Indeed, social life consists of all sorts of attachments and estrangements determined in part by this unconscious transposition and misidentification." [2]

The woman who shares deeply in her husband's call will want to be aware of what is going on in the world around her. What is happening as a result of the women's liberation movement, for instance, is definitely having its effect; there is a new woman in the pew. The families of the churches are being affected. What people do out in the working world affects the life of the church. Even the time of year and the weather has its effect. (Nineteen drops of rain will keep twenty Baptists away.)

The deacon with no opportunity to exert authority on the job may look for ways of doing so at church. The layman accustomed to telling others what to do at work may resist suggestions about how to get the job done at church.

People with family problems are bound to bring them to church and they can crop up in the most unexpected places. The man who is insecure about his job may be unhappy and overly cautious about congregational decisions requiring vision and faith.

Physical factors in community life have their effect. Churches on the growing edge of a city experience faster growth as a rule, than those closed in with no room for new people. One young pastor described to me the tremendous task he faced in seeking to reinforce and revitalize the life of a church shaken by staff difficulties, a changing racial mix in the neighborhood of the church, commercial zoning of property in the vicinity of the church, as well as an interstate highway which cut a swath across the area of the city where the church was located. Life on the outside definitely affects what goes on behind the stained glass windows in the worship and work of the church.

The method our churches utilize in securing pastors (and getting rid of them) intensifies our reaction to conflict. I suppose there are no perfect plans. A Methodist minister pointed out that in his denomination ministers experience conflict, too, but it may not be so traumatic because they know they will not have to live with it "forever." These men experience their own brand of stresses, however: unrest before the conference each year, feelings of being overlooked or bypassed, a sense of temporariness, and so on. There are political shenanigans in all denominations, I suppose.

> An experienced minister told us as a young couple, "The typical response of a congregation to a new pastor the first year is 'Here, kitty, kitty, nice kitty!' The second year it's 'Poor kitty!' The third year it's 'SCAT!'"

Knowing this to be fairly typical helps one accept evidences of waning popularity. Let's face it, television has created an expectancy on the part of congregations for performance on the rostrum, and a minister can soon lose his rating unless he has charisma and maintains a dynamic performance. Yet it is commonly agreed that congregations are much better served if they do not run through their pastors too rapidly.

What people think they want in a minister is not necessarily what they need, and maybe that is why God calls all sorts of men. Congregations are blessed when they realize that though some may wish for a different type of minister, God's man at the moment may be providing just the emphasis needed to make them a strong and beautiful church. It helps, too, if they recognize that congregations are imperfect, too, and success or failure can never be laid totally to its leadership.

It takes three years, some say, for a man to get to know

72

a situation well enough to give it the leadership needed. If the minister can get past the third year, he usually can stay a number of years.

> My husband has often reminded me that while conflict is not designed for our hurt, it does provide a testing ground for our faith. He also has reassured me that some conflict within the church is not his personal battle, but rather the Lord's. These thoughts have helped me put things in perspective when I have worried about the problems of the church.
>
> We found laughter indispensable when our congregations were plagued by conflict. When we thought we had absolutely nothing at all to smile about, we would "bare our teeth," pretending to smile at each other, on the way to church—and immediately break into real laughter. I firmly believe God has given us laughter for daily use.
>
> Another help he has given us is work to be done. We have retreated for a time to lick our wounds, but we never tarried long. There were always things to be done, people with problems so much greater than our own, people seeking help; and turning away from thoughts of self, we would find rest and relief in service.
>
> Time, we have found, is the greatest of healers. Hurts that keep on hurting for a long time finally are eased. God is good in giving us this healing.

All conflict is not caused by other people. We create a lot of problems for ourselves. We make mistakes. But no need crying over spilt milk. Blake Westmoreland has written, "I doubt if any person is wise enough always to do the best and most politic thing. The only thing we can set ourselves to do is to open our lives to the constant leading of God's Spirit, so that He who makes all things work together for good shall make this day a seed plot for a better tomorrow." [3]

In the normal give and take of a busy ministry, a solid,

sensible sounding board can be a great aid to stress prevention. Your observations of human nature may provide needed insights into staff relationships. You may detect symptoms in a counselee which your husband may not notice. Wild ideas sometimes need taming down; tame ideas often can be spiced up. A woman's point of view frequently has merit. Decisions made in times of discouragement—and sometimes they cannot wait—are not always reliable. Your husband may not always want your judgments, but you will probably find yourself sharing with him often in the lonesomeness of decision-making.

> Sometimes I have played the "devil's advocate" taking sides with persons opposing proposed plans, not because I was among the opposition but as a means of testing their point of view and the validity of the plan.

When a couple's relationship is strongly stable and there is mutual respect, they will find themselves both using that relationship for developing professionally. Everyone knows the value of having someone who will react honestly to opinions and ideas, someone whose point of view they regard highly.

Dr. James Taylor of New Orleans Seminary encourages his students to seek out someone to evaluate their preaching in terms of effectiveness, and he says some of the men are greatly helped by their wives' evaluation.

> During our seminary experience someone told me that the wife should never make a criticism of her husband's Sunday sermons before the following Wednesday. But this was never quite right for us! In fact, I have not found a just-right time.
>
> Dr. Taylor suggested that a touch of humor eases the pain of criticism and recalled once, as a young preacher, he was preaching on Abraham and kept saying "out yonder." Afterward his wife said dryly, "I thought if you

said 'out yonder' one more time I was going to get up and go out yonder!" He says he never forgot that.

Now and then I feel I should remind my husband to watch the length of his messages and recently, during lunch, the perfect opportunity arose.

I had made a nice little skillet of cornbread and as he cut it, he remarked that he liked his cornbread thinner than that. I replied, "Sometimes I feel like that about your sermons—there is a little too much between the crusts!"

Really, the criticism of creative effort is a delicate business at best. Writers coming to terms with the rejection slip and an editor's suggestions have to develop a strong sense of self-worth. They have to believe they are not being personally rejected. The same holds true of the man up front at church. It is great if he can take suggestions about how he might get his messages across most effectively without feeling personally rejected. Noting strong points—the good introduction, the appropriate illustration, the appealing conclusion—can counteract the sometimes adverse comment you feel you must make. It is easier to say nothing, to refuse to risk his misunderstanding your motive, but one wife puts it this way, "Before I let someone else criticize my husband, I try to be tactfully honest about weaknesses I see."

A tape recorder can be an asset to the man in ministry. If the preacher, listening to himself on tape, goes to sleep somewhere between the offertory and the benediction, he has evaluated himself.

Professional competence, you will recall, was one of the elements Dr. McClellan mentioned as characteristic of pastors who do not perish in the parish. Wives who care encourage their husbands to take advantage of continuing education opportunities, if they need a boost in this respect.

The cassette tape is an excellent way for these men to keep up professionally, for a lot of listening can take place on the road. Retreats, conferences, and seminary extension courses offer professional updates. Sometimes it requires a wife's sacrifice, in terms of family time and money, to take advantage of these opportunities.

> I continually marvel at my husband's ability to produce messages at the rate required of a pastor. I could never do it. And I have often wondered how the man with scant knowledge of the Bible keeps up with his sermon preparation. He needs a strong background of theological knowledge and a continuing input of information and inspiration to keep his presentations fresh and meaningful. He does not have the time to wait until the creative juices flow, until the mood strikes, to prepare his weekly messages. Like other professionals, he must do a good job even when he does not feel like it, and he needs the preparation of a professional.

And, of course, he must have time to give undivided attention to study and prayer. If you have been involved in making a creative presentation of any kind, you realize how essential concentration and uninterrupted time can be in the preparation process. Pastors who try to study at home need wives who help protect that time.

Sometimes they need a protector away from home. The wife of a Missouri pastor laughed about how her husband had gotten hung up with a counselee following a worship service the evening before they were to leave for a convention. She had gone on home to finish packing and when he finally arrived he demanded: "Where *were* you? She had me cornered!"

One of the greatest sources of stress for the man in ministry is the impossible task to which he is dedicated. Counselors are trying to help young ministers understand what they will face. Dr. James Cooper of Texas Baptists Ministers' Counseling Service told Southwestern students in a chapel message: "Learn to live with the impossible task. It can't be done. Accept it as that. Do the best you can, and leave the rest to God."

He pointed out that some men in ministry tend to deny their humanity, refusing to accept the fact that they can just do so much.

> Long ago I resigned myself to the fact that my husband was a slave for the Lord. Reading the Scriptures I realize that is really what Christian servanthood is all about, and I do not know anyone or anything I would rather he be committed to. A part of my personal commitment to the Lord is my commitment of my husband to his service, with whatever inconveniences and difficulties it may present for me. But I have provided practical reminders along the way. "Do you have to go?" I would say. Or, "Look, brother, I am your wife." Or, "You are an equipper, remember? You can only do so much yourself."

One thing we tend to forget, it seems to me, is that the gift of ministry is for the equipping of the saints. Granted, it is often easier to do it yourself (or to enlist your spouse), but the untouched potential in every congregation is appalling. It is a known fact that people will do no more than is expected of them. It is a shame when a congregation gets the idea they are paying their staff to do what they themselves ought to be helping to get done.

One of the most hopeful signs in our denomination for the relief of undue stress in ministry is the motivation and equipping of deacons for sharing in the pastoral ministries of a church. As I wrote in *On Being a Deacon's Wife:*

> One does not have to stand around a busy church office very long before it is clear that many of the calls coming

77

in cannot be neatly categorized under any one person's or organization's responsibility. The wife of an alcoholic, an unemployed executive, one teenager hooked on drugs and another at a stalemate with his parents, a bereaved husband, a divorcee looking for a job, a transient family of ten looking for housing, a shabby old man needing a few dollars to tide him over . . . . Who can help? Who will help? . . . By no means is the pastor always the man best prepared to meet the need of the hour, nor will time allow him personally to meet each need coming to his attention . . . [4]

Besides, it is impossible for the minister to continue to give strong support to families following crises because scarcely has one crisis demanding his attention passed before another crops up. There is definitely a limit to the number of persons to whom one can minister in-depth at any given time. If we are serious about reducing the stress level of ministering men, lay persons must be called upon to help get the job done. Also, we must get rid of the notion that the church has not ministered unless an ordained minister has personally appeared. The deacon family ministry plan, being promoted by our denomination, is seeking to develop this idea.

A missionary "Mrs." pointed out that one of the greatest stresses upon the man in ministry, and particularly the missionary, is the fear of failure. "Our men are being paid by God's people, and I think they are terribly uptight about this. In mission work, particularly, where the work is so slow, they may not feel they are really earning their pay. They think, 'For heaven's sake, I couldn't write down one statistic—nothing—to say, This is what I've done the past two years.'"

She noted that there is sometimes a tendency to guard oneself against getting into a position that has a lot of failure potential. "You see, the minister feels he is supposed to succeed, and even though he knows this may not always be a reasonable expectation, it's a kind of plague, something that's always there."

She went on to describe a decision she and her husband were facing, an offer of a position that, as she saw it, had all the potential for failure, yet a job that needed doing.

"I have to keep saying to my husband, 'I believe in this job and its value.' At the same time he needs to know that I realize it may fail and if it does, it's OK with me.

"You see," she went on, "if it's very important to a wife that a man 'succeed' and he knows she's all uptight about his position, that's going to be a hindrance to him.

"But," she pointed out, "there's worth in a job that doesn't look successful. There are sometimes dirty jobs to be done for the Lord. In a lot of cases there is ministry that has no visible results. Take a missionary doing village evangelism. He talks to one or two people in a day and gives them a Bible, but he hasn't done anything to boast about or to report. There's no building to show, no strong and growing relationships to reassure the outsider that missions has been done. It's just a job that we're commanded to do, a job that needs doing, and in some parts of the world it goes very very slowly; it takes days and weeks and even years."

> I think of the thousands upon thousands of tiny churches across our nation. Families needing ministry, young persons needing motivation, all needing a leader and a place of worship. Nothing that will set the world on fire, but work that will keep the torch burning for our Lord. "Lord, help us not to seek the spectacular in our service for thee. Help us to see the beauty and the perfection in the small things you have created and, seeing, to realize that in the smallest gatherings of your people, beautiful, meaningful, worthy things can happen."

79

With this understanding we will know true success for what it is, and we will provide our men with what may be most important of all to them: a good feeling about themselves at home.

Our trust will see them through all sorts of trials. As Dr. W. C. Tyler used to say to the young women in his classes at Blue Mountain College: "Girls, your husbands can stand the loss of material substance and make a comeback. They can stand the loss of one of your children by death and still survive. They can even give you up by death, no matter how much they love you, and keep on living. But the one loss they cannot overcome is the loss of your trust in them."

> Our daughter says a police officer's best backup unit is not his partner, nor the men who come hurrying in their car when he calls for help. She believes that, though she is never at the scene of the crime, an officer's best backup unit is his wife.

When man the minister steps into the pulpit or another place of ministry he goes alone except for his God. But fortunate is that God-called man who, either in reality or in his mind's eye, catches a glimpse of his wife's smile and knows that she cares enough to share with him in handling the pressures inherent in his work. She is indeed his best backup unit.

Notes

[1] Reprinted from *Wesley Christian Advocate*.
[2] Karl Menninger, *Whatever Became of Sin?* (New York: Hawthorne, 1973), p. 199.
[3] "It Might Have Been," *Rocky Mountain Baptist*, October 10, 1975.
[4] Martha Nelson, *On Being a Deacon's Wife* (Nashville: Broadman Press, 1972), p. 16.

6

Retreat—for Renewal

"I know I'm busy and all that, but I tell you
I do *quality* visiting with Mamma when I'm at
the house" (Jerry Clower).

The weekend has been called America's "moment of
hope." The average employee can count on fifty Satur-
day-Sunday breaks from his work, a hundred days a year
besides his vacation allotment. Many Americans are now
working a thirty-five hour week, and the four-day work
week is a reality for others.

In an effort to keep up with the times, church leaders
are delving into studies of the new leisure and Christian
uses of it.

Meanwhile, families in church-related vocations are
realizing their need for a pause in the midst of the pressure.
A survey of pastors' wives conducted by the Research
Department of the Baptist Sunday School Board found the
main pressure point of those surveyed to be "lack of time
together." A student at the New Orleans Seminary con-
ducting a survey among student couples heard the same
outcry, significantly more from male students than from
their wives.

It is time we take a hard look at what happens when
we permit ourselves to be taken over seven days a week

81

by work, whatever that work may be.

When what we have to offer is less than whole and less than Christlike, when we are too often irritable and weary, too often angry with our fellowman, when spouse and child alike express resentments about the work of church, then we need to back off and see if something may be wrong with the system.

When young persons embarking upon church-related careers see little hope for themselves as persons in the future, and when lay people express pity for us, we need to get a perspective on what we are permitting this shared call to do to us.

How can we handle its responsibilities and still live normal, wholesome lives? First of all, we must come to terms with our God. Nothing is more strongly stated in the Bible than the stewardship principle: we are managers for God. Surely this applies to church leaders and the way they manage their responsibilities, their energies, their time and their personal relationships.

It is an all-wise God who has broken time into its many segments. One of the first things our Creator did was make morning and evening. Day . . . night . . . weeks . . . months . . . seasons . . . years—all provide for the shutting away of the past and the opening of life to new beginnings, for a retreat from work and a return to it, for rest and recuperation and the renewal of physical, mental, and emotional powers.

The seventh day respite from work is a clearly stated biblical principle set out at the very beginning of time. God worked for six days, backed away to see that what he had done was good, and on the seventh he rested from his labors.

Having set an example, he then proceeded to command that man make a regular practice of sabbath observance.

Apparently he saw that the sabbath command would need more emphasis and reinforcement than some others, for in Exodus 20:8-11 you will note that ninety-four words are used to detail it. Only four are used for his command about murder.

Our Lord recognized the need for retreat for men in ministry. Listen as Jesus speaks: "Come ye yourselves apart into a desert place, and rest a while" (Mark 6:31-32). Mark goes on to explain why: "for there were many coming and going, and they had no leisure so much as to eat." So, at their Lord's insistence, the disciples went away in a boat to a deserted (uninhabited) spot where they could be alone.

Here we find the God of heaven initiating retreat—for renewal. "You fellows have got to get away! Let's get out of here for awhile."

What do you suppose Jesus and the men talked about as they left the beaten paths of Palestine? Did he spend this time teaching them difficult spiritual truths? Did he go over with them what they had done wrong and how they should go about ministry in the future? Or, leaving the scene of so much activity and so much talk of heavenly matters, did he encourage them to let the cares of a troubled world gradually slip away, to laugh together, to be comfortably silent, to let their eyes casually sweep in the beauty and peace of the hills and the sea that surrounded them?

God commanded the day of rest, and his Son kept the Jewish sabbath. He also saw to it that his disciples left off working for awhile to rest.

Yet many men who spend fifty Sundays working feel guilty about taking a day during the week to rest from a long week's work. Many who do lay aside their work for a spell feel they must sneak away, hiding the fact of

83

their need for rest as though it were sin.

Not only must we admit to God's wisdom and design for balancing work with rest, we must admit that we are human, physical beings with mind, emotions, and a body that will react somehow or other when mistreated. We must realize that no one can go on indefinitely working a seven day week, evenings included, without running into problems of one kind or another.

> Take it from us—we tried. A missionary friend visiting in our home in those early years warned, "You're going to burn out at this pace!" (We understand *he* burned out!) Both of us have spent our share of time having physical checkups and most of the time our aches and pains, particularly mine, have been stress related.
>
> My husband finally realized that he had to take some time off every week (not counting pastors' conferences). He has requested a day off wherever we have gone, and we are much more comfortable taking care of personal matters in time we can call our own rather than squeezing them in here and there, all the while wondering what people might think.

Your husband may have discovered that he has to negotiate for a day to call his own. Many congregations have not given a thought to the minister's need for it. If they have thought at all, they may assume that he has time on his hands between services! I believe congregations need to be made aware of the kinds of things that command a minister's attention between Sundays.

Now, assuming that we have some time to call our own, without feeling guilty, what shall we do? Two marital and family therapists have identified the troublemakers in a marriage as time, money, and space. They note that these are complicated by couples who have the notion that everything must be shared. They believe couples need to think in terms of "I" as well as "we." For the couple with children there is still another consideration. So, in planning for retreat for renewal, keep in mind the need of the individual to withdraw from daily pressures, the need for the couple to spend time together, and the need for the family to retreat.

Ashley McCaleb, the wife of a Mississippi minister of music and youth, calls the personal retreat for renewal "playtime." "Whatever is 'play' to you is what you do. Whether it's working in the yard, running out to the mall, getting off to yourself with a good book, or enjoying an old movie on television all by yourself."

Ashley's doing graduate work, but now and then she declares herself a holiday. "When I have a letup, I may play all week long. My neighbor Carol and I may take a gourmet cooking class, or we run back and forth to talk every day. Kind of like in a dorm. You see, we're close. I couldn't do that with a lot of people because I'd be afraid they'd take advantage. Sometimes we go for two or three weeks without seeing each other."

Carol is a member of another denomination, but in one church it happened that three of Ashley's closest friends were members of her church.

"If I did have a soulmate within the church, I wouldn't think anything about having her over to the exclusion of others. Having real close friends shows we are human beings with needs like other women. I guess there are people some places who get jealous, but I haven't observed this in churches we've known. I suppose it depends on their degree of pettiness. Now I can see if you run a friendship in the ground and neglect the church . . . or if you're always playing rook together . . . always sitting together or talking in a corner at the church . . . always seen together around town, it could be a problem. Adolescent-type friendships that require constant daily care might

85

not set so well with others . . . . But I wouldn't want that; I'm not that type person."

A youth director's wife from Oklahoma, the mother of a small son, said, "Time alone is my saving grace. Some of us need more than others, and I believe we've got to get over feeling guilty about that."

She takes a day for herself, gets a sitter, fixes her hair, goes shopping. "It's hard to feel rested," she said, "when you're cooped up with a two-year-old day in and day out. Some days you wish for a two-story house so you'd have taller walls to climb . . . . And you can't sew every day of the week. I don't want to sew all the time!"

Her church has a regular "Mother's Day Out" to meet the needs of others like herself who need retreat. "It's a hassle," the mothers declare, "arranging for transportation, getting the children up to the church, changing plans when there's a runny nose, and so on, but it's great fun to look forward to and some of us have become much better friends."

Churches with preschool day-care ministries are a godsend to caged-in parents; some have a drop-in setup in addition to regular care. Some mothers work out reciprocal agreements where they alternate keeping the children in order to give each other some free time. And, of course, one of the fringe benefits of being a minister's wife is being surrounded by loving, generous people who may be enlisted to help. Husbands, too, need to be called on from time to time to help provide the wife with this much-needed "I" time.

> The kind of time a woman needs for herself changes over the years. When our children were small I looked forward to the forty-minute nap instituted by my mother, a time when everyone in the house rested quietly after lunch.

86

My daughters recall my "Evenings In" when they were growing up: Mom all freshly bathed and powdered, propped up in bed, favorite magazine in hand. The door was shut but never locked to a daughter wanting to talk, and some of our best just-between-the-two-of-us conversations took place at these times.

Today I can spend hours moving things around in the house, puttering with houseplants, working in the yard. I walk two miles almost every day with two friends. I was ordered by my physician to build up to a mile a day, but these eager beavers (one twenty years my senior) were already hitting the trail for two miles, and they slowed down until I could take it. It is good for the nerves, as well as the arteries. I would rather spend forty minutes in the fresh air than in a doctor's waiting room.

Dr. Kenneth Cooper, developer of the aerobics exercise program and overseer of a preventive medical center in Dallas, said to a Southwestern Seminary audience: "Some of the most deconditioned people we have coming to our center are people associated with the ministry." *Southwestern News,* reporting the presentation, said Cooper's wife noted three reasons for exercise: rest and relaxation, figure contouring, and cardiovascular conditioning (this last most important, even for young adults). "It's incredible for me to think that you people are training yourselves to go out all over the world and preach the good news and you may not have a vehicle to get you there. You can train your mind and have so much to give, but if you die, what does it matter?"

Whether it is tennis or golf, jogging or cycling, a swim at the Y, or a workout at a health spa, exercise is great for retreat. Opportunities for diversion and retreat are all around us.

At one time I became interested in PTA and found this to be a retreat from overwhelming concerns about our church. In Denver I took advantage of an evening class in creative writing and joined two organizations of professionals in the creative arts—writers, poets, artists, and musicians. I have found that when you have an interest, you have the basis for friendships with women of varying ages, backgrounds, and interests. Last year, to escape the midwinter doldrums, I talked my husband into joining me in learning "How to Become a Travel Expert in Five Weeks."

"I" time, you see, is doing what you want for a while, and sharing it, if you like, with someone whose company you enjoy. It can restore dissipated energies, give you a more realistic perspective, make you more objective about your problems, provide much needed diversion for your mind and restore your mental and emotional equilibrium. It can chase a case of the blues and put a smile in your life.

It is yours for the asking, and with a little resourcefulness even the very busy and financially limited woman can manage it. But you have to take it; no one is going to hand it to you. If you do not, you may feel cheated and not really know why.

A man needs his "I" time, too, a fact wives often are reluctant to acknowledge. He too needs a chance to loaf a little, to golf or play tennis or putter around as he pleases. It is not always easy for the minister. A young pastor said to me, "With four kids eleven and under I feel guilty fishing on the reservoir. Time for family is so badly needed."

But I am convinced more and more that the Lord would not want his servant's time so limited that there is just none he can call his own. When a man retreats behind his newspaper or gets so absorbed in a television program he does not hear what you are saying, he may be expressing his need for a bit of privacy. He may be merely demanding his fair share of "I" time.

Likewise, children need their privacy. It is so easy for PK's to be programmed to death. More than others, they are deluged with friends and invitations, and they may have to be protected. They need some unstructured time that is their very own.

But it is a wise couple who realizes that not only is "I" time a must but so is a time for being together as a couple. Because of the extensiveness of our position, and the highly irregular hours, it is something we must work at scheduling. Dr. Drakeford said, "The minister and his wife have to get away from the idea that they are always on call. Like other married persons, they need some time alone, sometimes without even the kids around."

Dr. Rowatt emphasized: "Love is a product of time. We love someone we spend time with. If we don't spend time with someone, the relationship of love begins to fail . . . ."

Our husbands preach it all the time!

On-the-go couples may enjoy nothing more than a daily togethering at home, however. A counselor says every couple needs time for debriefing, every day if possible, a time for sharing what is going on, what each other needs to know, and so on (in our work almost like a staff meeting). But real togethering as a couple is not taken up with the business of the world beyond themselves.

When you have experienced togethering, you know it. It may happen walking across campus, holding hands . . . watching television together . . . sitting in a swing, shoulders touching . . . driving home from somewhere, the affairs of others' lives set aside for the time, conscious only of each other. It always takes the two of you. Sometimes you just happen upon it.

When I worked in St. Louis, we were a one car family,

and Carl usually drove me to work and came for me. Here, unexpectedly, during our very busiest days, we had time for each other. Those fifteen-minute drives became our togethering time.

Occasionally after work we planned something special. Once we took an unforgettable walk in Shaw's Gardens. Except for a gardener or two, it was all ours, our own Garden of Eden.

But such time may have to be definitely scheduled. A foreign missionary said his wife let him know early in his career that she needed some time with him each day, and over the years they have made a practice of sitting down and visiting with each other after lunch. Others speak of coffee break togethering. Some wives meet their husbands at their office and go to lunch together once or twice a week.

The master bedroom offers daily refuge for the minister and his wife. Here, of all places, a couple should be able to retreat from the stresses. But, being praying people, we often take our problems right to bed with us. Bedtime prayers, one counselor says, should be prayers of thanksgiving.

Dr. Rowatt believes couples should spend at least a week of their vacation together "and not at the Convention!" Just the two of them. "They owe it to their children, as well as themselves, to spend time alone together."

Twosome vacations can be delightful!

In recent years we have taken several economy vacations, replete with Coleman stove and picnic basket: a late May tour of Colorado; a canyon vacation in the West; a ferry trip to Victoria and a drive through western Canada up to Banff and Lake Louise; a return to the Florida Keys, renewing memories of our first year together; a week at the ocean, with miles of North Carolina beach to call our own. Dear as children and grandchildren are to us, and limited as our time with them is, we admit to a deep need to be away, alone together, for a while every year.

We do not make a practice of packing the burdens of our people into our vacation bags. Of course, we do not forget; sometimes we call to check. But we know that if vacation is to do its healing, we must do our part by clearing mind and heart for new experiences.

Mini-vacations, or pocket vacations, are ideal for the couple with small children still at home. They have the advantage of being less expensive and simpler to plan, and it is easier to arrange care for the children. They offer variety. Even a day off can be stretched into a mini-vacation by leaving the evening before and coming in late the next day. I hope we will someday see congregations granting three-day "R and R's" (similar to the long weekends so popular with the laity) to their staffs every few months, so they can take a real breather between vacations. Some ministers and their wives would value the time more than the additional salary.

Dr. Rowatt believes, as do many others concerned with family life, that ministers and their wives need a date by themselves at least once a week.

One couple in ministry found they enjoyed midday dating. On special occasions like an anniversary he takes off a little early at noon and they go out to a nice place to eat (prices are less then, they remind us). Then he goes back to his office at about 2:30. Many churchmen use their flexible schedules wisely to include the kinds of retreat they and their families need.

On our twenty-fifth anniversary we faced a usual workday with the Wednesday supper at church (which turned out to be a surprise celebration). I got up a few minutes early and prepared a breakfast which I billed "as different from anything we'd ever had or would probably ever have again." Using wedding china, crystal, and silver, we dined upon strawberries and cream, little sausages, and dainty rolls, with even a candle (at that time of day).

Granted, it takes some creativity to get a date with a minister, but where there is a woman there is a way.

Some couples in ministry like to spend some of their precious tohering time double-dating. Eight or ten Nashville couples, for instance, get together monthly for dinner out and dessert in one of their homes. It is an unspoken law that talk of church and related matters is taboo.

> On our return to our home state we were delighted when we were invited to join three other couples for supper every six weeks. The hosts provide the meat and extras, and the others come with a vegetable, salad, or dessert.
>
> Last time they were at our house we spent a whole dollar and a half to take them paddleboating in the moonlight on Pelahatchie Lake.

Groups like these can be formed so easily and can do so much to alleviate some of the loneliness God's servants and their wives experience. We cheat ourselves when we do not cultivate one another on a non-professional basis.

Not only do couples need retreat, but also family retreats are a necessity if MK's and PK's are to grow up normally. It is a shame for children to be brought up feeling there is never any time for anything else in the world but church.

> We picnicked so much when our youngsters were growing up that I thought I would never want to see another picnic in all my life. But then I learned about quiknics. Just grab whatever is at hand and put it into a picnic basket. Lay it out on a redwood table or an old quilt, garnish with sunshine, top with blue sky, sprinkle with a bug or two—and you have a quiknic.

One young woman with her three-year-old packs a quiknic occasionally and meets Daddy in a park between their home and his office on his lunch hour.

Parks, lakes, boats, campers, tents—all are aids to retreat. One ingenious couple turned an abandoned school bus into a stationary camper, with built-ins, running water, a porch swing under a canopy, and a tiny landscaped lawn.

A "place" can make retreat simpler. It creates strong memories, can save time, money, and often disappointment. A busy banker we know has a lakeside cottage only a mile from his regular residence. He and his family run out often to fish and swim and boat; it is so handy, they say.

> A Missouri game warden helped us find a "place," an abandoned one-room schoolhouse on a creek which ran into Black River. My, the memories we have of our Springhaven (or "Tick Dock" as we dubbed it at times): exploring, wading, floating, shooting the rapids, fishing. A family weiner roast on a gravel bar. Frog legs and hush puppies cooked over an open fire in a misty dawn beside Cool Pool.
>
> Even in Colorado, where you can drive in a different direction every week for years and still fail to see it all, we had our places—"Singing Rock" on the South Platte; Echo Lake at the foot of Mount Evans—places to which we returned often, with ever increasing pleasure.

Some families may opt for greater variety. Anita Thorne described the diversity of their family retreats: picnicking by the Sea of Galilee; camping by the Red Sea at Christmas and Easter. "We have a tent and we really rough it," she said. "Sometimes we go to Jerusalem to look at biblical sites, or down in the old marketplace, or to an art gallery. We go to Haifa for an occasional Walt Disney movie. We bowl, we play tennis, and sometimes go to the "Y" in our town.

"Sometimes I have to say to my husband, 'We're going.' We cannot always wait until he feels free. It's something I've had to work at over the years, and my husband does see now that it's important. If you just wait and wait, you may wait forever!" Thoughtfully she added, "It's harder for the men to turn loose than for us."

This family has taken their Arab neighbors, with children the ages of theirs, camping with them in Greece. "We don't feel it's mission work, for these are our friends. It's a joy to see things through the eyes of those who have not gotten out into the world so much."

Family retreats should be a priority item for the family busy with church-related activities. At times the church, well-meaning though it is, seems to pull the family apart with its age-level activities. Parents sometimes have to call a halt, even if it means someone missing one of its worthwhile activities in order for the family to have its togethering times.

Our Lord has set the example for retreat. He took his "I" time, drawing aside to pray, alone. He retreated frequently with those closest to him: Peter and James and John; Mary and Martha and Lazarus. And he and his larger family, the twelve, we are told, retreated for renewal.

The life of the disciple in church-related work today is strenuous. It is no brief dash for glory. Like long-distance runners, the ministering couple must pace themselves.

Walking with Jesus, someone has said, means letting him set the pace.
"The Lord is my Pace-setter,
    I shall not rush;
He makes me stop and rest
    for quiet intervals.
He provides me with images of stillness
    which restore my serenity;

He leads me in ways of efficiency
  through calmness of mind
And his guidance is my peace.
Even though I have a great many things
  to accomplish each day,
I will not fret, for his presence is here.
His timelessness, his all importance
  will keep me in balance.
He prepares refreshment and renewal in the midst of my
  activity
By anointing my mind with his oils of tranquillity.
My cup of joyous energy overflows.
Surely harmony and effectiveness
  shall be the fruits of my hours
For I shall walk in the pace of my Lord
  and dwell in his house forever." [1]

Notes

[1] From *PSALM 23, Several Versions* compiled by K. H. Strange, published by
The Saint Andrews Press, Edinburgh.

7

Love at Home

"Clergymen and their wives have some unusual battles to fight in achieving happy marriages, but they also have unusual access to resources for help" (G. Lloyd Rediger).

A Christian home is a great treasure in our time, and none has more potential than that of the ministering couple. But, as you know, the very foundations of our nation's homes are being shaken, and the minister's is not exempt. In addition to the problems besetting every family, the couple in the church-related vocation soon discovers that the work imposes unique strains.

Thus we have a challenge: to create a workable marital relationship and to develop strategies for wholesome and gratifying family living.

Marriage to any man is a challenge, and especially if he is a minister! At a Mississippi Baptist Pastors' Retreat, following my talk, "The Wife in Your Life," Dr. Herschel Hobbs laughingly told the audience that on their forty-eighth wedding anniversary, his Oklahoma City church presented Mrs. Hobbs with an orchid—on a purple, heart-shaped pillow, with this citation: "Any woman who's lived with Herschel Hobbs for forty-eight years deserves a Purple Heart!"

In talking with five marriage and family counselors in preparation for writing, I said, "I think I know what our problems are. My question is, What are the answers?"

Since the work tends to affect our homes so deeply, they began by identifying the occupational hazards of the ministry. "It is the nature of the preacher to be rather demanding because of his prophetic role in the church," Dr. Drakeford said. "It's not easy for the pastor to shuck this off when he moves into a domestic role."

An usher at the Southern Baptist Convention in Denver had made a similar observation. "These men are accustomed to telling folks where to sit, not being told!" she remarked.

Like the law enforcement officer who sometimes may treat his wife and kids like suspects, the preacher may sometimes tend to treat his wife and kids like sinners.

Of course, the work can be demanding. As one preacher said reflectively, "What other man in the world besides a doctor or a minister gets an emergency call while he's making love to his wife and is expected to leave her and go minister to another man's wife?"

These men can be very preoccupied. An Arkansas leader laughs about the young minister at the marriage enrichment retreat who runs about, notebook in hand, getting all the help he can to take back home to help others, completely oblivious of his little wife who stands shifting from one foot to another in the shadows. "She needs him, but you can't get his attention to tell him so."

They tend to exhaust themselves in service. A man in religious education said to me, "We have to be so self-giving on the job, when we get home we just don't want to be bothered."

Dr. J. Clark Hensley of the Mississippi Baptist Christian Action Commission finds some typical work-related attitudes in those who come to him for crisis counseling. These ministers in trouble may be operating on one or more of the following assumptions which he has dubbed as: (1) The king can do no wrong; (2) I have to set everything right (sometimes called the messiah complex); (3) The Lord will provide without my common sense, good judgment, or planning; I'm a child of the King and I'll live like a prince; (4) A golden halo for the preacher and a little tin halo for his wife; and/or (5) The slightest wish of my most neurotic, self-centered member is my highest command.

Some who come to Hensley for crisis counseling have been playing the numbers game, seeing how many "spiritual scalps" they can hang at their belts. Others have fallen prey to what he calls "Baptist Baal worship," making an idol of their position in the name of the Lord, making a thing of their spouse to achieve goals, enhance image, or lift their status. One thing these men have going for them is the fact that they are seeking professional counsel.

"But what's a wife to do?" I kept asking, anxious lest I come away without any answers. A Texas wife had looked at me blankly on learning what I was writing and asked, "What are you going to say?" And a Presbyterian from Colorado had written resignedly, "I've made my peace by recognizing that unless you get a man when he is three years old, you haven't a chance . . . ."

All of the counselors said that a wife must take some positive steps. "You've got to call on these men to see themselves as family persons, to help them put things back in perspective . . . . The wife must use her influence . . . . Somehow you have to get his attention . . . . The wife must demand her fair share of the marriage!" Years before I had heard a St. Louis psychologist tell a group of ministers' wives to get down in the middle of the floor, if necessary, and kick and scream to get husband's attention!

98

But Dr. John Drakeford, director of the Marriage and Counseling Center at Southwestern, countered. "I think a woman has to use a bit of finesse. I don't believe she'll get her way with strident voice. Rather than standing up and demanding, I believe she has to be a bit gentle—soft, but firm."

Each of the counselors expressed a great deal of concern over the effects of certain widely publicized philosophies of Christian marriage and their overtones for wives of men in ministry.

Dr. Bertha Bunda, director of social services at Hinds General Hospital in Jackson, Mississippi, put it plainly: "I'm concerned about these courses in 'submission.' Every time I see a sweet young thing trying to follow the instructions, I know that somewhere out there things are going to collapse; there's going to be an explosion. She is simply burying feelings that must be worked through."

The strong emphasis upon equality for women has brought about this counterrevolution. Basing ideas on biblical texts, sometimes quite irresponsibly, some women are urging wives to pretend submission, all the while making secret decisions and attempting to control the husband's sexual behavior. Some even go so far as to tell the woman how to dress and when and why.

Men trying to set the wives on the right path are focusing strongly on a male dominance theme, a hierarchy of authority or a chain of command. Some of the plans appear to place unreasonable demands upon God; others, unreasonable demands upon the husband as well as the wife. Rigid roles for both husband and wife are outlined with specific detail.

Now there is a great deal about Christian submission to be found in the New Testament, but I find some of the current interpretations of the husband-wife relationship foreign to the example and teachings of our Lord.

Granted, there must be a leader in every situation (and there are many opportunities for leadership of one kind or another in marriage). But the finest leaders do not dominate. They frequently do not even have to delegate. Like Jesus, the best leaders give freedom to those with whom they are associated, freedom to make choices, even mistakes, freedom to express themselves, freedom to develop their gifts.

> In a pillow talk one evening my husband shared with me a satisfying interpretation of Ephesians 5:24-25, Paul's comparison of the husband-wife relationship to Christ and the church.
>
> Because we are so much involved in the Lord's church, the parallel was highly meaningful to me. We know that Christ does not dominate his church, forcing his will upon her. Even though he is the head of the church, he leaves her free to choose her responses.
>
> With this in mind I understood better the ideal Paul presents. The husband's love is to be patterned after Christ's love for the church. The wife's submission is to be patterned after the church's yielding to the will of the Lord.
>
> What a beautiful portrayal of responsibility and freedom. Any interpretation that results in the husband dominating his wife and the wife becoming a nonperson is a radical departure from the Christ-church pattern.

Young women of my generation were on their own when it came to relating to their husbands. There were no popular books, few articles, no cassette tapes or courses on the subject. Not many preachers ventured legalistic interpretations to the passages of Scripture now so in vogue. We were left to our own resources, with little more than intuition as a guide.

We read Paul's admonitions to wives, interpreting them within the framework of our particular marriage and the times and culture in which we lived. If we promised to obey our husbands (we'd have agreed to almost anything in that romantic glow), our obedience was probably closest to the word's Latin derivative which means "to listen to."

It worked for most of us. With our husbands we struggled toward oneness, giving a little, taking a little, misunderstanding sometimes—at our best, yielding to one another out of love.

We were wed for better or for worse and we did what we could to make it better. Divorce was rare. Leaders debated about permitting a divorced person to teach in the Sunday School. And divorce for a couple in ministry? Unheard of. We believed that marriage was meant for a lifetime.

There were times when some may have thought, guiltily, that it would be easier to go it alone. But we didn't dwell on the thought. As one preacher said jokingly when asked if he'd ever considered divorce, "Divorce—never! Murder, occasionally!"

> At our house we arrived at unworded agreements about who would make the rules in certain areas of our family life, what the rules were and who would enforce them. For instance, I was in charge of the household. Husband brought home money for food and clothing; I took it from there. I paid the bills and kept us out of the red week by week; he did tax reports and kept us solvent annually.
>
> He was the family authority on matters spiritual. He took the lead in family worship.
>
> I handled the discipline of the children when they were with me; he took over when he was on hand. I tempered his strong sense of rightness; he balanced my easier-going nature. When I tended to be harsh, he was gentle, and vice versa. As our teenagers tugged for independence, we tried to present a solid front, not always without struggle.

101

There were no pat answers to married life back then, and I would venture to guess there still are not. Like sets of fingerprints, marriages are unique, no two alike. Each needs the very best creative effort both partners can bring to it.

Every marriage needs a good communication system. If the couple is going to balance the many differences each brings to the marriage, they must exchange thoughts, ideas, and feelings. Communication takes place through love-making, listening, and a coming to terms with one another over differences, frustrations, and anger.

Wives know only too well that when all is going well in one aspect of the relationship, all else goes better, too. We cannot readily turn off our negative emotions of anger, hurt, and frustration. Unless they are aired, communication in our most intimate moments suffers.

Complicating matters for the Christian couple is the damaging idea that anger is wrong and should be hidden. Dr. Drakeford notes that a lot of marriages get off to a bad start at the seminary level. Wife works all day; husband has his excuses ready for leaving as soon as supper is over. But, as one wife said dryly, "If you went over to the library, you'd see him sitting there with those cute little coeds, and I'm back home with a sinkful of dirty dishes. Everything is more important than me!" The wife continually buries her anger and resentment, fearing reproach or thinking it would be sinful to express it. Feelings backlog; eventually a crack in the foundation of the marriage develops, and there is sure to be trouble out ahead.

Our interpretation of the word "Christian" may need to be reevaluated, Dr. Edge commented. "We say to ourselves and others that we must try to make our homes 'Christian.' Of all places where we ought to be Christian, it is in our home with people we love.

"But when you come home, you have been nice and kind and loving and 'Christian' all these other places. You've got to have somewhere you can be real. And how are you going to be real *and* 'Christian'?

"Where can you let off some steam? Somewhere you've got to do this . . . . I have in my own being a real conflict in trying to be 'Christian' and real," he said. "It looks like we could be Christian and real all at the same time."

And then, thoughtfully he added, "Maybe what we've called 'Christian'—loving and accepting, never angry, never frustrated—is not really what it's all about. There are times when you want to blow up."

> Some of the protocol inevitable for pastors and their wives bothers me. I know it is not nice to admit it, and I know my husband does not enjoy my saying so. But he allows me to, and it certainly makes me feel better to groan and complain, "Oh, no, not another . . . ."
>
> He knows the feeling, too. He comes in angry—it has been one of those mornings; he has held his tongue, but now it must come out. In turn, I must permit him to be real in my presence.

This is what counselors call open communication at the feeling level, and it is needed, particularly in the minister's family where feelings run high at times.

Victor Frankl has said that an abnormal reaction to an abnormal situation is normal behavior. Look at Job—did *he* ever react! And our God understood.

Dennis Guernsey, in his book *Thoroughly Married—Sexual Communication*,[1] notes that anger can be expressed in two ways: assertively or aggressively. For instance, the wife may say assertively, "I'm feeling neglected." Or aggressively, "You have time for everyone but me!" The husband may say assertively, "This house is a mess!" or aggressively, "You're a lousy housekeeper!" Learning to express our anger assertively, we can defuse it without misbehaving too badly.

Communication is work. In busy families it must be planned for. It needs the kind of attention that a little child demanded when she turned her mother's face toward her and said, "Think about me, Mommy, nobody but me!" It takes time. But, as one busy couple asks, "What kind of a god would create persons male and female, place love in their hearts, call them into holy matrimony, and then begrudge the couple the time it takes to keep their love alive and growing?"

If couples would clarify their expectations of one another some of the conflict could be avoided. For instance, the husband needs to define clearly his time commitments. "A wife can put up with a little time if she realizes that's all she's going to get," said Rowatt. "But if she's expecting tons and it comes in a matchbox, then she's disappointed. Disappointment is not always determined by how much, but how much in relation to what is expected . . . . Sort of like a lean Christmas—if you know ahead of time, you're not so disappointed."

Now and then, though, someone or something is neglected and it takes a confrontation to clear the air. It is easier to pout, but it is more loving to confront. "Carefrontation," someone has called confrontation-in-love. It takes a kind of tough love to call your beloved on the carpet and run the risk of being misunderstood, even momentarily hated. But there are times when both husband and wife will need to say to the other, "Hey, look here, we've got to do something about this . . . ." And while you may run into some resistance, the confrontation will likely result in some adjustments.

One couple in ministry has observed that "such balancing is a periodic maintenance task of the marriage and can never be permanently achieved. Equilibrium is a delicate achievement which requires sensitivity, alertness and honesty."

In a letter to the editor of the *Baptist Program*, Don S. Burnett shared an excellent example of a wife's confrontation-in-love. He had just returned from a long string of revival and church engagements during which his wife had struggled bravely to meet their sons' need for both father and mother.

As we sat down together she said, 'Honey, don't you see? The church here will probably have many pastors over the years. What you're unable to give to some need or opportunity, another man can provide. But the boys and I have no other father or husband to give us the love and interest, the support and fellowship we crave and so desperately need. If you fail us, no one else in the world can make it up.

" 'You may not accomplish all for Christ you desire in this church, but there are many churches and many years ahead in which you can reap a great spiritual harvest. But when our boys are grown in a few short years your opportunity as a father to influence and shape their destinies will be over. It is *now* or *never* for them!' "

Mothers, as well as busy fathers, may occasionally need a reminder that the children in the home need some personal attention. It is difficult for anyone whose work is highly engrossing to juggle time and psychic energy to include both "I" time, "we" time with a spouse, and time for the children as well.

When one is weary it is so easy to say, "I'm too tired," or "Keep quiet," but the possible consequences of consistent neglect are frightening! I wept as I read a letter from a pastor's wife: "Our children are all grown now . . . . We have never really had a husband and father . . . .

Now only one of our five children attends church regularly . . . . O God!"

The remarks of children can break your heart, comments like "You're no daddy! You're just a going away man!" or (at a family picnic) "Like always. Everything we do is in the middle of." (After a funeral, wondering what he would do for a daddy if his Daddy died) "I wouldn't want Mother to marry another preacher—preachers are never home"; or (from a prodigal son returning): "Dad, the only time you ever had for me was when you thought I wanted to be saved. I faked a conversion experience just to get you to show me some attention."

Dr. Hensley admitted that it jarred him when his five-year-old son called his office one day to ask for an appointment to talk with him. He does not recommend exploiting the child to jolt a very busy dad to attention but he does insist that the mother go to bat for him.

Dr. Rowatt urged, "Say to the wives that ministers need to help with the tasks of parenting. Their kids have loaned their father to everyone else. Other kids have a father.

"The significant moments of transition in our children's lives are too often set aside in favor of other things that may seem important, but which in the realm of eternity are so unimportant. It is sad to hear a young woman say, 'My father wasn't present at any of my graduations—eighth grade, high school, or college. He never came to any of the ball games. When I was crowned queen in our little town, my dad never showed up.' "

Rowatt said, "If the minister's wife can nail him down and get him to these events, she'll be helping him."

Of course, there are sometimes unavoidable conflicts. At a conference last fall I watched a denomination leader obviously hurting. Several states away, his son, a star athlete, was playing the big game of his senior year. That dad wanted to be there, but he had a professional commitment and he had no choice.

We have all observed families in public life who have shared a strong commitment to servanthood with the husband and father and whose youngsters seem none the worse from wear. But not all couples are bred to that kind of battle nor are they willing to take a chance at winning the world at the risk of losing a child.

Observers of the minister's family frequently remind us that more children of ministers go on to be listed in Who's Who than children of any other professional. But the role of minister in our time has so changed that only time will tell its long-range effects upon the children.

Not all ministers and their wives have difficulty managing time for love at home, of course. One said, "We have never made a big to-do about Dad being away nor tried to compensate with expensive outings. Our children remember what might be called insignificant times spent together." In the unhurried moments of family living a great deal of sharing, listening, and loving can take place.

When the need is immediate, these parents call a halt and take the time to meet it. In one home a pastor and his teenage son had reached a stalemate, and the gap was widening. One Wednesday evening they had begun talking at the dinner table, and the father realized that at last they were making progress. It was right at prayer meeting time, but he went to the phone, called a deacon at the church, explaining, "I've been detained and I won't be able to be at church this evening. Will you carry on for me?" Probably nothing that the father said had as much effect upon the son as did that action.

There are times when mother, too, must make similar judgments to meet the needs of a child.

James Barry of Nashville tells a beautiful story of love

at home. Dr. L. R. Scarborough excused himself from a family gathering one evening in order to prepare for a chapel message. In a little while he heard a knock on his study door and his little grandson entered. As Dr. Scarborough laid aside his papers and reached for the boy, the child said, "Granddaddy, we've gotta have a little lovin' around here!"

The next day, the story goes, Dr. Scarborough gave one of the finest talks he ever made. He called it, "We Gotta Have a Little Lovin' Around Here."

A little lovin' goes a long way in a godly home. One little boy went along with his busy father to his office one Saturday evening. As they made their way through the darkened building to a light switch, the child squeezed his father's hand and said, "I love you, Daddy. You know the way."

When the spirit of love dwells in a man and his wife, and when they take the time to translate that spirit into the daily relationships of family, there is love at home.

Notes

[1] Dennis Guernsey, *Thoroughly Married—Sexual Communication* (Waco: Word, 1975), p. 40.

8

Love at Church

"Men are often brave and good alone, but they
are never really effective unless they share in
some kind of group reality" (Elton Trueblood).

In a recent survey of pastors' wives, conducted by the
Sunday School Board's Research Department, 80.9% of
respondents agreed with the statement, "Pastors' wives
should be trained for their special responsibilities."

Dr. Bunda believes that ministers' wives need training
in relationships, as well. "Because it's a lonely role," she
observed, "the wife tends to depend more upon her husband and immediate family than the normal wife. In his
position, the husband cannot give as much support as she
may need, and all too often she just goes to pieces." (She
told me that among professional wives only doctors' wives
seem to have more need for counseling than ministers'
wives.)

"You wives need a consultant, someone with expertise,
someone to be objective, with knowledge of the structure
of your churches, to help you bring things into perspective.
You need ongoing support, someone to work with you
systematically at intervals. You particularly need someone
who can say, 'You're succeeding.'

"Why don't churches put something in their budgets

for this kind of program?" she asked me. "There are lots of good counselors around. But there doesn't seem to be any kind of system whereby ministers' wives in a given area can sit down together and ventilate with somebody. If they had such a system, the women would find friends who would in turn be supportive of one another."

> As a young woman I was utterly innocent of both the responsibilities and relationships that would be mine in church life. I believe my husband and I both would have benefited from an orientation in which we would have considered together, as a couple, the implications of the call to ministry.
>
> Then, while he was learning to preach, I needed a study in human relations, especially those such as one encounters as a minister's wife.
>
> I have needed help at the feeling level along the way—practice in handling the demands, slights, and criticisms that all ministers' wives eventually encounter. I needed to learn how to cope with the emotional strain of being so closely associated with the hundreds of hurting persons who reached out to us for help across the years.

The point of the wife's greatest need, however, is in the realm of theology. Dr. Clifton Perkins of Mississippi Baptists' Church-Minister Relations office, says pulpit committees are by far more interested in the wife's attitude toward her husband's work than anything else. We need a deeply rooted, basic good will toward the church and a firm recognition of its need for leadership to see us through the difficult days which seem to be par for the course.

The theology of church, of course, cannot be absorbed in a single session. But how vital that we understand from the outset what the church is all about . . . .

That it is a plan, with a 2,000 year history of remarkable success.

It is people, affirming their identity as Christians, seeking reinforcement and support.

It is a group acknowledging its need for leadership and authoritative spiritual guidance.

The purposes of the church-in-meeting are worship, learning, fellowship, and service. The purposes of the church-scattered are witness, influence, and ministry.

The facts of church life take time for the learning:

A church is a family of brothers and sisters. Its meeting place is its home.

Ideally, the church is the saved—a group of individuals bound together by a common love for the Lord Jesus Christ.

Realistically—well, let us put it this way: the shock of reality hits when the minister and his wife discover that there are more than two kinds of people in the world; the saved and the lost.

For the church is made up of believers, all of whom continually battle the sinful bodies in which the Spirit of Christ dwells.

Within the ranks of these believers are many immature Christians, some still in the nursery of the Christian life. Some are children in terms of spiritual growth, and some behave as unpredictably as adolescents. Many peripheral members relate to the church family like distant cousins. They are absent from the family reunions and are scarcely known.

Then, there are those of the family who are out of sorts with everyone; we say they are "out of fellowship." Some of these have attached themselves to leaders of the past and have become disenchanted. Some have put their faith in fellow members more than the Lord and are disillusioned; some have suffered real hurt at the hands of fellow believers.

Also, on every church roll—and God only knows who

and how many—are the unredeemed, some well-meaning but unaware. Some have moved in with the family for selfish reasons; others have been urged to join and have been heartily welcomed by family members.

And, of course, on every church roll are the dear hearts and gentle people.

> At times Carl has said he would rather minister to a collection of such saints (these maturing, loving, receptive people) than to receive a collection *from* the saints!

But more important to our theology is the conviction that the church is the body, the bride, of our Lord Jesus Christ.

> In a message to our congregation, Chester Swor appealingly illustrated the urgency for a warm, loving relationship with the church. "Suppose you have a son you love very much and this son brings home a beautiful girl to be his bride. If you don't love that girl, something comes between you and your son." Even so, something comes between you and the Lord if you have reservations about his church.

We in the Lord's work bask in such beautiful thoughts, but the church is a working situation which calls forth diligence, determination, and perseverance.

> Out West we learned that there are two kinds of ranches—dude ranches, which cater to vacationers, and working ranches. After we had been in Colorado for a while, members of the church outfitted Carl with authentic Western wear, saying, "You've been around here long enough for the real stuff!" Before presenting him with a fine pair of Western boots, they handed him a joker—a pair of old cowboy boots so dusty and scuffed you would have thought they had walked right in from a working ranch. Sometimes I display them in our den with some dried grasses. They symbolize so well our bout with the West.

112

Not only is a church a working situation, but, to borrow from the Western vernacular, you ride what you draw. At rodeos the cowboys in the bucking contests do not get to choose their animals. They have to ride what they draw. If the animal does not respond, the rider cannot really show his skill.

The Lord's man comes prepared to his position, but he may be inhibited in his performance if his congregation does not respond to his leadership. Some congregations are stable and strong and mature. Some are immature, weak, and wavering. Some are adventuresome. Some balk at the very thought of change.

And to carry the comparison a bit farther, the pastor and his wife had better ride loose in the saddle but be prepared to hang on when the going gets rough.

A certain professionalism is required in our working relationships, the wife of a minister of music and youth reminded me. She had had a rude awakening when she had to submit an application in writing to her husband for the position of church pianist!

"It's hard to treat your husband like a director, not a husband," she said. "We have to have poise and dignity. If we're going to fall apart, we have to wait 'til we get home." Some choirs, I have heard, have been embarrassed by the obvious conflict raging between piano and platform.

A husband who sings professionally with his wife acknowledged, "If you work with someone whom you're not going home with, you probably could be more objective and not get as emotional." He noted that a man and his wife will have different ideas on style, timing, and selections much as any other two performers.

Inter-staff relationships are obviously among the most trying assignments the ministering couple is handed. A church staff is composed of men with some of God's special gifts. Dr. Roy Fish, in a taped exposition of Romans 12:14, makes an interesting observation that wherever Paul discusses special gifts he follows immediately with strong admonitions to love. This may indicate that the potential for problems is inherent in the possession of the special gifts for ministry.

Too many staff relationships have foundered. In one case communication between a pastor and a minister of music degenerated to note writing. When the wife of the music minister became critically ill prior to childbirth, the pastor did not so much as inquire. In another situation a staff member sought counsel about some family problems from the pastor, and the pastor turned on him, refusing to allow him on the platform from then on. Dr. Hensley notes that certain pitfalls of the pastorate—despotism, professionalism, and commercialism—can seriously affect staff relations.

On the other hand, some staff men working with a pastor also suffer certain temptations: to be lazy, subversive, indiscreet, and unethical—so much so that there are pastors who vow they will do without rather than take a chance on further staff trouble.

Wives can sometimes help their husbands do better. The wife may be able to be more objective. She may be able to bring some balance to a tendency to think more highly of one type of ministry than another. When things get tense, she may be able to temper her husband's feelings and call upon his deepest convictions about Christianity in action. There are inevitably two sides to staff problems, and both parties may have to swallow their pride and bring their best spiritual resources to the need for harmony.

It is not easy for a wife to keep her cool when she knows too much, one wife pointed out. "It's hard to listen to a sermon knowing what I know. It's hard to worship, all the time thinking, 'You big fake!' To have a good relationship with the Lord in spite of what's going on in the office is a tremendous challenge."

It is trying for staff wives whose pastor's wife is a prima donna, First Lady type. "You know," as one put it, "that you'll never be more than 'second lady.' " One observer of the church scene remarked that she had not seen a great deal of compassion on the part of pastors' wives for staff ministers' wives. She believes the relationship between these women depends on how well the pastor's wife can disengage herself from an ego trip. Ideally, these wives reach out to one another in Christian love. Deep friendships and family-like relationships sometimes develop.

It is a wise wife who recognizes that the church is her husband's bailiwick and leaves the bulk of the work and the worry to him, but the woman in the one-man church may find herself thrust into the position of an assistant-of-sorts. "These churches need what a wife may be able to offer," Helen Alderman said. "There are so many details to keeping a church going, and most pastors' wives are equipped to offer excellent assistance. The wife is likely to be up on what is going on in the denomination and has the know-how for improving leadership, physical facilities, materials and equipment; she is approachable and knows how to be sympathetic."

We hurt ourselves when we cringe at the thought of working for the Lord. After all, so many of us are trained. Our loyalties are not likely to be divided. But we have to appropriate the time necessary to do the work, or we will be thoroughly frustrated.

The pastor's wife may assume a kind of unauthorized leadership role (and at times lay it down), depending upon her inclinations and at the discretion of her husband and herself. Love at church is seeing something that needs doing for God and helping your husband get it done without trying to take over.

> In churches we have served I have observed that the women tend to look upon me as a sort of resource person. It would never be my choice but apparently I am considered a part of the package marked "Pastor." I wish they would not, but in groups some who speak up look toward me for affirmation when they venture an opinion. Others call to me for answers and I try to be helpful but I do not speak for my husband.
>
> I have been asked, "Who is this Lottie Moon? Did she have a fire?"; "What do you mean 'covered dish?' "; "What does the word stewardship mean?", and a thousand other questions.
>
> When I get edgy from too many and too much, I cry out to Carl that it is time for retreat—for renewal.

Every profession has its public or its patrons. A church has its people and here is where love is often put to the test. The sooner we accept the fact that churches are made up of imperfect people, working with imperfect plans in a world that is trying its best to cause them to fail, the better off we are. Likewise, there are all sorts of Baptists around the world and we cannot afford to be personally insulted every time someone says something negative about the denomination or the church.

Personalities are going to clash; your husband's ideas will not always be welcomed (and this hurts, for ideas are like babies, none quite like your own). There will be clashes between the old and the new—but after all, suppose those were *your* toothprints on that second pew: you would not want the building bulldozed either!

If what I am told is true, there is a power structure (obvious or otherwise) in every church.

> Nobody told me it was par for the course for the pastor and the deacons to differ at times. I thought all should be sweetness and light at church. But I have found out that it is not just my husband who runs into problems with the power structure.

A pastor understands that his is a call to lead. But there is a strong belief on the part of some deacons that their job is to keep the leader under control. Some tell him in no uncertain terms. Others hint at it. Still others can be ruthless in their determination to overrule his every suggestion. Many, however, could not be kinder or more cooperative and helpful.

In reply to a Southern Baptist Convention leader who asked Dr. Perkins which one thing brought most pastors to his office for counsel, he said by far the most common problem is conflict with deacons who consider themselves a board of directors. The "board" concept (under which deacons screen items of business, consider pastor and staff responsible to them, and must approve use of finances and facilities of the church) is certainly not scriptural. The early deacons were chosen to unify that early church and to minister to evident needs.

On the other hand, some deacons have to put up with a lot. One spoke of that "young whippersnapper preacher boy who thinks he knows it all and wants to change everything around here." And it has occurred to me that some balking deacons may have saved their church some embarrassment by speaking up as they did against some wild idea cooked up in a ministerial ivory tower.

Some of the difficulties ministers run into are inherited: cliques, divisions, monstrous building debts, strange doctrine. Both minister and wife may inherit ghosts from the past. One wife said her predecessor was a real troublemaker and gossip, careless with her charge accounts, and

117

so on. As the next pastor's wife, she had to prove herself before she was accepted. (Not much worse than trying to succeed an angel, probably!)

Acceptance of a minister is not automatic, either. I have read that it sometimes takes two or three years or more for the transfer of affection to take place from one minister to another. This is prolonged if a former minister continues to maintain close relationships, returning frequently for weddings, funerals, visits, etc. While it is too much to expect members to stop loving a former leader, we can hope that they will readily accept new leadership.

In hopes of doing away with some of the ghosts, I remind deacons' wives that the very differences in spiritual leaders can help develop a strong church. A writer in *Pastoral Psychology* says, "If the congregation can accept these differences, much like one accepts design, pattern and color shading in the beauty and richness of fabrics, then all concerned can beautify their lives as persons and as a congregation."

Every business and profession notes certain difficult-to-live-with traits in its public. In a young ministers' wives' retreat sponsored by the Woman's Missionary Union of Mississippi, Peggy Hicks, a Southern Seminary faculty wife, suggested to the wives that they might as well learn to live surrounded by discontent. "There will always be discontented people, wherever you are." This may be because we as Christians are preoccupied and, rightly so, with ideals and thus are ready victims for discouragement and disappointment. Whatever the reason, we do have to learn to shrug off the barbs, sift what we hear, and not bother our husbands with every little thing. A little professional toughness comes in handy at times.

As long as there are members who leave you with a sense of being owned by them, there will be the need for wives of ministers to know how to handle their comments and demands. The girl who has grown up in a large family where she has had to fend for herself, or one whose parents encouraged independence may find it simple. But she will find the Spirit-fruit of gentleness, kindness, and self-control real assets as she lives within the context of a local church. The need to be real is no excuse for being harsh, cruel, inconsiderate, or uncaring.

You may be one of the vast majority, however, who has difficulty expressing feelings, beliefs, and desires honestly, directly and appropriately. It is essential that you develop this ability, for only as you do can you be your own person, in command of your life rather than subject to the whims and desires of others.

This is not contradictory to the Christian teaching of meekness. Meekness has been defined as "under the dominion of our Lord, our strengths and personalities submitted to him." It is possible to be pleasantly firm and quietly decisive with dignity and poise. Of course, everybody is not going to like you, but that will be true no matter what you do.

Groups of wives might benefit by adapting principles in the field of assertiveness training to gain experience in knowing how to make requests, to say no, to answer put-downs, and to engage in feeling talk. To practice, one woman could role play the problem situation, with several others responding spontaneously, while the rest of the group rates their responses as "too inhibited," "not inhibited enough," and "well done."

Take these situations, for example:

• A young mother is worried because she has seen someone repeatedly kiss her baby in the mouth.

• Your telephone rings regularly at 9 A.M.; it is a member who "has problems and needs to talk."

- Your husband is a minister of youth, and some teenagers have begun stopping by your apartment often; they stay late and raid the refrigerator before they leave.
- A member reminds you that she and her husband "not only have to pay our utility bills, but we pay yours, too."
- You are invited to a luncheon, and you are exhausted from having house guests for the past week.
- Your husband is a minister of music. A member complains to you about "the music our young people are singing."
- You are called on the carpet about your husband's interpretation of a certain Scripture and you do not have the theological background to defend it.

Usually threatening confrontations come without warning. There are no two alike, and there is no time to prepare. You need to be in good shape physically and spiritually to be able to handle them confidently. I believe there is definitely a cutoff point as to what you can afford to say, because more harm than good results when we unnecessarily antagonize or alienate persons our husbands are trying to lead.

Nothing compares to good, sound common sense in handling the people-situations of church life. As one wife said so wisely, "If we will just accept the people, even as we expect to be accepted . . . . The people have the right to be themselves, too. They have the right and the need to be comfortable at church, and we must let them be what they are. We have come a long way when we can respect their commitment."

Work of every kind has its strains, but not all is typified by the constant barrage of problems that are a part of ministering through a local church.

"How does a wife learn to handle the emotional strain?"

I asked Dr. Carroll Freeman, of New Orleans Seminary. He advises us to be as objective as possible, to remember that the Bible teaches us, not only to bear one another's burdens, but also that each should bear his own burden. "You cannot afford to get emotionally involved, for you will find yourself overwhelmed and enmeshed by the problem. If you 'go native' you lose the objective stance necessary to counseling. You have to keep some distance."

> Carl calls it a stiff elbow. He has learned to handle the woman in the congregation who repeatedly hastens down the aisle to drape herself about him during an invitation. "I just stiffen my elbow to help her keep her distance," he says. It is a technique you have to use with persons who demand more than a fair share of your time, too.

And it is *our* time. We are responsible to God for our stewardship of it. Dr. Freeman notes that we have to be tactful, of course, and carefully weigh each situation. But you may have to say, "I have so many things to do—I'd love to talk with you, but I have other responsibilities, and my first reponsibility is to my family."

He suggests another technique for handling the over-dependent type. "Rather than letting them run rampant with their symptoms and take you over, say, 'Let's set aside fifteen minutes sometime to discuss these things that you're troubled about.' This puts you in control."

He noted that we tend to listen longest to those who talk the loudest and then judge them to be representative of the church. "You have to be frank with the person who's bending your ear all the time. Though you might think you're alienating the whole church, the problem personality may be known for this kind of thing."

Additional emotional strain comes if the minister-husband starts to project his frustrations upon the wife.

would be going a lot better than they are!") Dr. Hensley says we have an obligation to ourselves not to accept projection. He suggests the wife tell her husband, "I know you're frustrated and I want to empathize but I'm not going to accept responsibility for things that are not going well!"

Dr. Rowatt tells Southern Seminary students they have no right to use their wives as a garbage dump. The wife may sometimes have to say, "Stop. I don't want to hear any more. You'll have to get help somewhere else." He is a firm believer in professional counsel for the minister who is in trouble.

Dr. Hensley added a practical note, "Tell the wife to get a tune-up before she breaks down. She should see her doctor when things get too much for her. She is not God, and she must not allow persons to impose the burden of deity upon her.

"See your doctor and then follow his advice. If he prescribes a tranquilizer, take it," he advises. "Don't think because you're a special person of the Lord's, you don't need help at times. When used appropriately, under a doctor's prescription, medication may well be God's way of helping you in healing. To refuse to take such medication when needed is to refuse God's help."

I asked Dr. Bunda about the warning signs that a woman may need help. "When she is depressed and wants to stay in, away from things; when she is very angry without being able to put her fingers on why; when the feeling grows that she really does not want to go to church; when she begins to pick up on every little thing people say to her; when she is sick a lot with backaches, stomachaches, headaches; and when she cries a lot—these are signs she may need some medical help with the strain she is under."

It is hard sometimes for the wife to sort out the happenings of church life, and it may be painful, for what happens within this church body happens to her husband. The part of that body which is the minister is so strong, yet so sensitive. And when he hurts, she hurts, too, because they are one flesh.

> One Sunday I witnessed the kind of heartbreak so many experience at one time or another. My husband had led a revival effort in a tiny, struggling church in the Northwest. Following the final service, we were departing for a few days' vacation in Canada. We waited and waited and waited for the pastor and his wife to join us for good-byes, and at long last they appeared, a sag to their walk.
>
> "John and Mary stayed to tell us they are leaving the church," they explained. This couple and their children had been mainstays in that weak congregation, giving, serving, helping however they were needed. "But they have decided . . . ." (Many of you, I am sure, can fill in the reasons.)
>
> The wife, a strong, mature Christian woman, if ever there was one, broke down, weeping, and my heart went out to her.
>
> We went on our way, our vacationing mood thoroughly dampened, incensed to think that two professing Christians would use such ill-planned timing for such an announcement, and wondering why . . . why . . . why . . . .

As another wife said to me later, "Tell the people we love them but we do not always understand them." And another added, "There will be experiences that will defy understanding, so many things that are frustrating and heartbreaking, and there is nothing you can do but just stand by . . . just stand by, that is all . . . and know it is the Lord's church. It is the body of Christ and not our organization, and he is going to see it through in spite of our bungling sometimes . . . *usually* in spite of . . . .

"There are times when you'd just better pick up and go fishing!"

Nowhere in all the world is there more love—and more potential for love—than between the people who make up the Lord's church. Yet sometimes, surrounded by people who know how to love, and so many who need to be loved, one may feel lonely and unloved.

One afternoon as Helen Alderman and I talked, I think we discovered one of the secrets to love at church. "I found it as I worked in church music," she said, "especially as we practiced in small groups like quartets . . . . And in working with children. I got to know families through teaching their youngsters. Come to think of it, it has been the ordinary, everyday experiences which have drawn me closest to the people of the church."

As she talked, I thought of where I had found love. It was not necessarily among those who were most faithful in attendance, much as I admired their loyalty. "I found love both for the Lord and his people in the little gatherings that have dotted my life—in classes and committees and study groups and casual encounters in the hallways and walkways about our churches. I found it whenever I got interested in the members as persons, in what they were doing and how they felt and what life had dealt out to them, their victories and their losses."

Love at church, we decided, does not happen so long as the congregation remains a sea of faces. It happens in the small group situations that are a part of the magic of Southern Baptist life. It happens when one reaches out with the heart to meet another's need for friendship, reassurance, caring, and hope.

Herein is love at church.

9

Serenity Tips from Seasoned Wives

"God, grant me the serenity to accept the things
I cannot change, the courage to change the things
I can, and the wisdom to know the difference."

Early in my preparation for writing I began scattering
informal questionnaires among ministers' wives wherever
I went. While one replied, "I hate such thought provoking
questions," others took time to jot replies about how they
were handling some of the problems that plague even the
best of us. I am including some of the comments here,
and, because of limited space, have summarized others.

Time

Nothing has given me more cause for concern than my
stewardship of time. Recently I began what I call prayer-
planning, and this has settled my sense of frustration
immensely. During my early morning meditation I sort
of gather myself together for the day, read some Scripture
and talk things over with the Lord. Usually I write a little
prayer relating to the day. Frequently I sketch out a rough
calendar for the next few days and block out the time
already committed. Then, what is left I clutch to my heart!
I have "first class" time and "economy" time, calculated
on my mental and physical peaks, and I like to go first

class with the things that need my best efforts.

On the questionnaire I asked how some change of attitude, action taken, or technique utilized had helped others in the matter of time use, and here are some of the replies:

- HELP!
- Never have enough hours in the day!
- We use every minute of it!
- I have learned to do chores as soon and quickly as possible and not put them off. Still trying to learn to plan ahead.
- Since I work, everyone helps at home. I have to budget my time.
- I suppose I have cheated myself; just had to make ends meet in taking care of missionary, home, and family responsibilities. I have not thought about many of the things I would "like" to do.
- My life is so full of things I enjoy doing that this is a real problem. It takes real planning, but I try to organize so I can get the most important things done first.
- We try to make the most of what we have. I am trying to learn to let David relax around the house instead of always wanting to go somewhere. I try not to do housework and laundry when he is at home.
- We think *Time for All Things* by Charlie Shedd should be required reading for every pastor and his wife.
- I am a disorganized person, but I have found listing the day's activities in priority order and doing the most important things first a great help.

The Energy Crisis

At times I have been spread so thin I was coming through in spots, so one of my questions was "How do you avoid a sense of spreading yourself so thin?"

- In our first pastorate I tried to *do* and *be everything!* Even

sing in the choir, when I could not ᵉ
I gradually realized I was not being a
my abilities and so I have learned to

- I used to try to be all things to all people
  I was asked. I cried a lot. Learning to
  best thing for me. I am happy now with
  I try to do as much as is reasonable.
- I have learned to say, "I cannot handle tha‌
- I know my limitations and give a good explanation when
  I say no. I am learning to live with my answers without
  feeling guilty.
- What I can do, I do, and what I cannot I leave off,
  even if it upsets my husband. I know my limitations
  and have to live with them.
- I either do without something or use dollars I earn to
  pay for a few hours' household help. A local home
  economics teacher has been an excellent resource for
  students who want to work.
- We love our church and try to do as God leads but
  do not believe he expects us to push ourselves until
  we cannot go. Deacons are supposed to help.
- If you do not have the time or the desire to do something,
  it is better to say no and have someone else mad at
  you rather than for you to be mad at yourself.
- After many periods of bad health (most of them stress
  related) I realized I could only be myself, one person,
  and strive to do the most important, most valuable things
  for my family, the church, and the Lord. I learned to
  pray about situations I could not improve and let God
  work (it takes some a long time to learn this lesson).

Children

The following were responses to the question, "What
are you doing to help your children have a healthy attitude

father's work and the church?"

not tell Jonathan that Daddy has gone to *church* during the week; rather I tell him Daddy is at work. On Wednesdays and Sundays we go to *church*. If we happen to stop by during the week, we go to "Daddy's office."

- We found new insights into growing children in *Promises to Peter*, by Charlie Shedd, tried them and found them good.
- We try to help them realize that father's work is a very special calling of God.
- We are trying to include our children in our call. We share with them as we can and let them help. We encourage them to express their ideas and we include them in our sense of accomplishment.
- We have tried to teach them to be concerned about people. I have genuinely enjoyed church life and church folks myself.
- We have never shared our fears, doubts, criticisms, or church problems with the children . . . . We came to the place with our youngest where we just loved him in spite of himself and turned him over to God. Praise God! His grace is sufficient! Our son is married now and has just given his life to God to do whatever he wants with it.
- The children and I realize that people who go into the ministry are above all human themselves, and the church is made up of similar persons—seeking, searching, and contemplating life's meaning, its joys, and the answers for its sorrows.
- We tried never to teach them they must do or be certain things because of who their father was. They did develop some resentments at being expected to be better than other children because they were PK's.

128

- It is easy for missionaries to comment on problems of colleagues and expressions of the nationals in such a way that the children lose respect for them. We try not to carry on this type of conversation before the children. We talk frankly, if necessary.
- Our boys used to ask if there would be committee meetings in heaven. They have understood since early days that the Lord's work comes first. But their daddy never was one to schedule something every night of the week.
- We pray for families in the church by name and need.
- I try to be honest about my feelings with the children. I show my disgust, joy, pride, and frustrations and discuss a lot of my problems with them, for this is life. I think it has helped them see us parents as human, and yet realize that the principles we hold important are not going to change. I try to point out the good, no matter how bad the situation.
- Our children still get a little upset about church members calling us home from a vacation. They seem to accept the other happenings. We have tried to point up the positive. After learning about a move, our eight-year-old went off by himself. A long time later he said, "I guess we will go and find some more people to love."

The Identity Crisis

Probably we can make every adjustment more readily if we feel free to be ourselves, so I asked others to share how they have gone about finding and maintaining their self-identity:

- No use trying to be what you are not. Even children can see through that!
- I had to stop trying to be the ideal pastor's wife and

129

doing the things I thought a pastor's wife ought to do.

- I determined to be a Christian first and then a minister's wife. This has helped the church people to not just *use* me.
- I just remember I am *me* as the Lord has made me.
- I am not a perfect person and I have to do the best I can with the ability God has given me.
- Living in a metropolitan area, I find there is not quite the problem of maintaining self-identity as in a small community.
- I have consciously tried not to become proficient in my husband's field of work. I have learned not to be uncomfortable over being considered a "strong" character who has definite ideas about things.
- Every day I say to myself a statement by Karl Menninger: "It is a good mental health practice to find a mission that is so much bigger than you are that you can never accomplish it alone. A task that takes thought and energy; a mission for the common good." I always stay involved in such a task.
- By developing some interests of my own, doing things at church in which my husband is not involved, going places alone or with friends, I feel a little more like my own person instead of my husband's shadow.
- Through working I have an outlet for my abilities. My self-esteem has been raised tremendously. I no longer feel I have to do everything everyone asks of me. I feel freer to let God give me leadership instead of being a people-pleaser.

Privacy

I was surprised at the number who indicated this was no problem. They "love people," "adore sharing with others," "cannot remember the time when people took advantage," and feel that people are fairly considerate and respectful of their privacy. One wrote, "It does not upset me if somebody comes by in the morning while I am still in my robe."

A few, in rural situations, indicate lack of privacy to be a continuing concern. "When we moved here, we were on an eight-party line. I could not even call home and cry to my mother! I could not start to town without someone wanting to go along," a young wife said.

Another wrote resignedly, "I just smile and try to love the people."

A counselor I talked with declares there are still situations where the parsonage has always been left open, and the appearance of locks is offensive—but "go ahead, put locks on the doors and use them," he advises.

Entertaining

There was a great variation in responses on the matter of entertaining, some noting that while they enjoyed entertaining in the past, costs have made it prohibitive. Some women who have a knack with the snack entertain often as part of their ministry to people. A few still stretch dining table and budget to include frequent dinner guests.

Some use their homes extensively as a center of Christian influence. Roe and Fran McClure, for instance, are the kind of folks to whom people looking for a home away from home just gravitate. Fran turns over her kitchen to a coed wanting to cook a meal for an out-of-town boyfriend, lends her guest room to a student between semesters and feeds chili by the gallon to youth groups. Even on vacation they are apt to attract unkempt strangers to their picnic table without so much as a "be our guest."

Other couples rarely have guests in. Their home is their

hideout, their oasis, their haven. They encourage people to see them at the church.

But many a pastor's wife and missionary wife has enough house guests in a lifetime to qualify her as a professional innkeeper. A pastor's wife laughs now about the time she had to farm out two children during a revival in order to make room for an evangelist and singer whom nobody else would take in. The guests did not like the room she had prepared for them; they watched TV past midnight and slept late; refused to visit; and lounged around the house all day making snide comments about the church and its members while her husband went on with his work and the visitation. As the week wore on, the evangelist began to hint around about his personal problems with sin and guilt and observed that "all preachers' wives were starved for affection." The music man, single, and every bit of twenty-one, had his advice on child rearing and even accused one of the PK's of going through his luggage.

Our "victim" went to bed the day after the revival, teeth chattering and body jerking all over. During the night her husband called a doctor who arranged for him to pick up some medication at a rest home. In all the confusion, she misunderstood the dosage, and after taking one sleeping pill every hour for three hours, she was knocked out good and proper. At his office next day, where she was taken limp as a rag, her case was diagnosed as nervous exhaustion.

It would be great if we could get some foundation to finance research into solutions to some of our "problems." Meanwhile, the welcome mat is out!

Problem People

Every life situation, I suppose, includes some relationships with problem people, so I asked how others were coping with those in their congregation:

- I let them know I love them but try not to get too involved. Keep just enough distance, and after twenty years you will know about how to handle them.

- Pray, pray, pray. If God's man is in God's will, God will send the messages the congregation needs for conviction. To me the only true answer is prayer.

- Love them all as Christ loved us. Turn the other cheek. Try to have no biases. Be firm, be truthful, have self-control, but love and let God work.

- We *try* to remember that each person is a person of worth. Bob can find a redeemable quality in everyone.

- I try not to be too critical (that's hard).

- I try never to harbor in my heart any wrongs that are done . . . . My husband is not one to talk about this kind of thing, and this helps.

- We recognize we are all only human. I try to rise above pettiness.

- I have tried to understand why people act as they do. You know that saying, about walking in someone else's moccasins for so many moons . . . .

- Do not be a listener of gossip. Stop it before it gets started by saying something good about the person.

- I try to search for a way to make these people part of the solution to the problem. Sometimes a little kindness and support can turn a "problem" into a "prophet."

- Be gentle.

- I have tried to see their side and turned them off if too unreasonable.

- Most of my dealings with this type have been as I served as a sounding board for my husband as he thought through the situation and how to deal with it. I tried to be sympathetic with him, but also looked objectively as possible on their side of the problem.

- This has been difficult. The best remedies I have found is: 1) try to understand the situation, 2) to try not to lose control, and 3) to pray.
- We have had some prize winners! Only through prayer and faith that God would see us through have I been able to cope.
- Love is the key. Start praying for persons and before long you will be concerned about them, and you can grow to love them in spite of their weaknesses.
- I can always find some good qualities in these persons.
- Prayer, acceptance, and forgiveness.
- I have always tried to be *direct* with problem people. I have gone to women who were hurting the church, themselves, or someone else, and talked with them about it, never blaming them but taking the attitude that I was sure they did not realize the problems they were causing. Sometimes they did, but I have given them the benefit of the doubt. Sometimes this works.
- Love thy enemy.
- We have learned to accept the fact that some are emotionally unstable and are going to cause problems for any pastor. We listen, decide if anything needs to be done, and if it does not, forget it. We also laugh a lot!
- We try to be understanding and helpful but realize that everyone cannot be satisfied.
- Often a "problem" can be turned into a friend and supporter if you can find a service the person can render you or the church and ask him to help.
- I try to do little things for people who have an ugly attitude toward us, and be nice to them.
- I recognize that sometimes Satan uses people.

- In a previous pastorate there were some people I could not cope with, and my husband had to do it for me. We may still be in a honeymoon here, but so far so good. A great church and some great people!

Disappointment and Disillusionment

I was interested in finding out whether other wives also experienced disappointment and disillusionment, and how they were handling these emotions. Their responses were reassuring:

- I try to be good and remember he is God's man and there will be better days, hopefully.
- During the initial stage I get by myself, review the experience, cry, feel pity, then remember the Lord is near. I wish I could learn to reverse the order.
- Long ago I learned to take people as they are, and then I would not be so disappointed. It helps to realize that everyone is human and not as angelic as they might appear at first.
- The two of us try to get things out in the open between us. Applying such Scriptures as Romans 8:28-29 and Philippians 4:6-7 has helped us over the hump many times.
- I tackle some physical chore.
- I remember the almighty God is still in control. The painful experience may turn out to be a blessing in disguise. You have to wait upon the Lord; do not run ahead of him.
- Some situations I just rode out! Many times I lived with the disappointment too long, prone to wondering what I could have done differently.
- The only way I have been able to cope is go home and pray.
- I am not good at handling these. Charles is worse.

135

My manner is to shut it up tight in the inside, and not talk about it at all. He talks about it more, and this is better for his emotional health. I let it lie, believing it will be healed eventually.

- I keep quiet and listen. I try to do something special, like making a favorite dessert for our dinner.
- These have to be given over to Christ for healing. As long as I harbor these feelings, they fester in me and affect my whole life.
- Face the situation, accept it, analyze why it happened. If you cannot help the situation, try to learn from it, pray about it, leave it in God's hands, and try to forget it (except for the lesson you learned).
- I pray. Philippians 4:6 is one of my favorite Scriptures (I call it my PST formula). I ask God to fill me and so surround me with his love that it will overflow onto others. That always gets me out of my doldrums.

One seasoned wife concluded with "It's not all sugar and spice, but if there is a lot of love in the home, there will be lots of love in the church, too. I know sometimes there seems to be a lot of sacrificing, but it is worth it all."

10

Be Confident, My Heart

"Let everyone bless God and sing his praises,
for he holds our lives in his hands. And he holds
our feet to the path" (Psalm 66:8-9).

It is impossible to communicate in this one small book
all the helpful suggestions that came as I studied the relationships and responsibilities within the call we share.
Without exception, the individuals with whom I talked
expressed interest in the undertaking, and agreed there
is a definite need for the couple in ministry to take a hard
look at the call, considering together what they will do
with it, what it will do to them, and what God may want
to do through them.

"Don't postpone happiness," Mrs. Landrum Leavell
urges student-wives at the New Orleans seminary, and
that is good advice for us all. "You can be just as happy
right where you are, struggling, as you'll be ten years from
now. You just don't suddenly get happy when you get
all the things you want!

"We've stressed the negative too long. There are so
many marvelous things about the Lord's work. Think of
the people you'll meet, the opportunities you will have,
and all that you and your children will be privileged to
enjoy, *because* your husband is a minister. Think on these

things . . . ."

Yes, it is true, to serve is to suffer sometimes. But I do not believe God wants any of us to suffer unnecessarily. I am confident he has placed within each of us remarkable sources for adapting to and coping with our circumstances. There is no doubt that his Word is filled with promises appropriate to our need for daily strength and reassurance.

Granted, no two marriages are alike, nor are any two congregations or working relationships. Solutions must ultimately be found within the creativity of the two of you, in your determination and your dependence upon the God who has tapped you for service.

> When God reached down and took over the life of my husband there in Pearl Harbor, he knew all about the young woman Carl Nelson had married. He knew she needed a Savior, and it was he who moved Carl to reach out across an ocean with those love letters that won me to the Lord.
>
> Knowing my limitations as well as my potential, knowing full well the struggles I would experience along the way, still God called.
>
> It was a call to share ourselves with some of God's best people on behalf of the greatest cause in all the world.
>
> I am a privileged woman to have been able to observe at such close hand our God at work in so many lives. While the world has acclaimed its Christian heroes, I have seen what God can do with quiet people in obscure places. My life has been touched by the faith, patience, kindness, and prayers of common folk who have ministered to us and have given us hope in the power and the purposes of the God we have served together. My heart has applauded as I have watched ordinary men and women become extraordinary by virtue of the nobility and courage with which they have endured their sufferings.
>
> Our life has been, and continues to be, as Paul Tournier puts it so beautifully, an adventure directed by God.

Only God knows the measure of one's ministries. Only

138

he can judge. But of this we can be confident: when God calls a man, he wants his wife to come along.

And surely there is no higher level of human sharing than that between a man and his wife, united in love, working together on an assignment handed to them by God.